Green Witch
MAGICK

Essential Plants and Crafty Spellwork for a Witch's Cupboard

SUSAN ILKA TUTTLE

FAIR WINDS

Inspiring | Educating | Creating | Entertaining

Brimming with creative inspiration, how-to projects, and useful information to enrich your everyday life, Quarto Knows is a favorite destination for those pursuing their interests and passions. Visit our site and dig deeper with our books into your area of interest: Quarto Creates, Quarto Cooks, Quarto Homes, Quarto Lives, Quarto Drives, Quarto Explores, Quarto Gifts, or Quarto Kids.

First Published in 2021 by Fair Winds Press, an imprint of The Quarto Group,
100 Cummings Center, Suite 265-D, Beverly, MA 01915, USA.
T (978) 282-9590 F (978) 283-2742 QuartoKnows.com

Fair Winds Press titles are also available at discount for retail, wholesale, promotional, and bulk purchase. For details, contact the Special Sales Manager by email at specialsales@quarto.com or by mail at The Quarto Group, Attn: Special Sales Manager, 100 Cummings Center, Suite 265-D, Beverly, MA 01915, USA.

25 24 23 22 21   1 2 3 4 5

ISBN: 978-1-58923-985-2

Digital edition published in 2021

eISBN: 978-1-58923-986-9

Library of Congress Cataloging-in-Publication Data

Tuttle, Susan Ilka, author.
Green witch magick / Susan Ilka Tuttle.
ISBN 9781589239852 (trade paperback) | ISBN 9781589239869 (ebook)
1. Witchcraft. 2. Magic. 3. Herbs—Miscellanea. 4. Plants—Miscellanea.
LCC BF1566 .T88 2021 (print) | LCC BF1566 (ebook) | DDC 133.4/3--dc23

LCCN 2021006338 (print) | LCCN 2021006339 (ebook)

Cover Design: Leslie Olson, leslielynneolson.com
Page Layout: Megan Jones Design
Photography: Susan Ilka Tuttle
Illustration: Shutterstock, except page 33

Printed in China

This book is an educational resource. The information in this book is not medical advice and is not a substitute for working with a health care practitioner. If you have a medical condition, take medications, are pregnant or breast-feeding, or otherwise need medical or herbal advice, consult your qualified health care practitioner before using the plants in this book. Always first test small amounts of a plant or topical preparations to see how your body reacts. Educate yourself about plant safety to correctly identify any wild food.

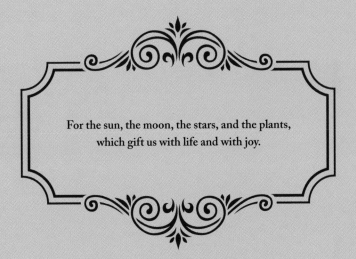

For the sun, the moon, the stars, and the plants,
which gift us with life and with joy.

Contents

INTRODUCTION

Plants. They provide us with clean air to breathe. They give us nourishing food and natural medicine to sustain and strengthen our bodies, support our minds, and feed our souls. Plants gift us with the essentials we need to live and thrive. In return, we protect Mother Earth and Her limited resources. This is the way of the green witch.

Humankind has always innately known and understood the healing and magickal powers of plants. Over time though, we've allowed ourselves to move away from this inner knowing—we've lost our appreciation for and connection to the natural world. Some even consciously choose to ignore and bury this sacred knowledge. Even so, this innate knowledge remains with us and is reawakening in a strong way among many people, especially as we see the harmful effects of our choices over centuries.

I am cautiously optimistic and also a realist, and I do believe this is truly an exciting time. So many more humans are becoming curious about and even embracing activities that have always come naturally to the green witch—things such as gardening, folk herbalism, responsible and respectful foraging and wildcrafting, and the spiritual practices of witchcraft. All of these invite us to return to our roots, reverse environmental damage, and reestablish balance and harmony.

It's encouraging to see these activities move from the fringe into the mainstream, creating opportunities for those who feel the calling—the green witches, naturalists, foragers, wildcrafters, herbalists, gardeners, and environmentalists. Many of them serve as luminaries to help reintroduce

our society, especially the young, to a reciprocal relationship with Green Energy. It's a birthright for all.

Reconnecting with plants is one way to reestablish our connection with Mother Earth. It is the way of the green witch and ultimately the goal of this book. Within these pages, we explore the individual, Earth-honoring path of the green witch. Working in partnership with plants is an integral part of this path. We get to know (remember) thirteen sacred, essential plants for the witch's cupboard—safe, healing plant allies that we can co-create with for medicinal, culinary, and magickal purposes. After we get to know them, we apply this knowledge in a hands-on way to make natural remedies, recipes, and magickal creations.

The thirteen essential plants in this book were carefully selected to include wild plants that grow readily throughout the world where people have settled. I have also chosen plants that can be cultivated easily in our own gardens, grown in a sunny window, or purchased from the market. And we'll become familiar with a handful of plants that grow in the wild and are also cultivated. I wanted to make sure that all readers, both city and country dwellers, have easy and safe access to a majority of the plants in this book. Some selections are quite practical but no less beneficial and powerful.

My intention for this book is to provide you with a guide to green witchcraft and to working in concert with plants that can support our bodies, minds, and spirits. It is my wish that my offering will help you forge a deeper spiritual connection with the life-giving, miraculous plants that grow

all around you. I hope that you will find a lifelong, adventurous journey of co-creating with plants—sharing your knowledge about them, caring for them, and preserving them as our planet's precious resources.

In this beautiful dance of reciprocity with Mother Earth, may we use our gifts to give more than we receive, to restore balance and harmony to the natural world of which we are a part, in exchange for the gift of the dance.

HOW TO USE THIS BOOK

Part I of this book introduces you to witchcraft basics, its roots, and the variety of paths that witches can take. We then turn to green witchcraft, of which working with plants is an important part.

The plant profiles in part II present thirteen sacred and essential herbs for the witch's cupboard—safe, healing plant allies that you can work with for medicinal, culinary, and magickal purposes. Each profile contains:

- Common name, scientific name, other folk names, and family name
- Astrology classification: the plant's ruling planet (including the sun and moon) and associated zodiac sign or signs
- Element correspondence: Earth, Air, Fire, and Water
- Plant lore, history, myths, stories, and legend passed down from generation to generation
- Identification traits and plant parts used
- Medicinal and culinary uses
- Magickal correspondences: the plant's vibrational powers in areas such as protection, healing, love, luck, or psychic powers

The profiles are intended to help you use herbs in your craft. Understanding their astrological, elemental, and magickal correspondences will give you insight into the energy and power of the plant. For example, plants associated with the moon are connected to peace, healing, sleep, and psychic dreams, and Air plants are connected with psychic powers, prophetic visions, intellect, and wisdom.

This book can be read cover to cover, or you can skip around according to your interest. Reading up on foraging and herbalism basics (chapter 6) will help prepare you for the projects in chapters 7 and 8. It's also helpful to reference the profiles of the plants as you explore the projects, to gain a full understanding of the plant or plants that you are working with.

After getting to know each plant, you'll work with them intimately in part III through the hands-on projects for herbal remedies, culinary recipes, spellwork, rituals, and divination practices. Explore the list of suggested resources. Each of the thirteen plants in this book can be used in spellwork that corresponds with their particular magickal properties. They can also enhance your divination practices, through both their magickal and medicinal capabilities. As you do these projects, please always honor your personal relationships with and feelings about certain plants, in addition to the traditional magickal correspondences given in the book. For example, if a rose signifies a sense of home and belonging to you, something that is not considered a traditional magickal property of this plant, embrace that personal association.

Food as Medicine

You'll notice that medicinal and culinary uses are offered in each profile. Keep in mind that there is often a fine line between what is considered to be a medicinal versus culinary use of a plant, and sometimes that line is completely blurred. That is because "food as medicine" applies to culinary uses of these healthy and nutritious plants.

Essential Oils

Did you know it takes sixty roses to make just one drop of rose essential oil? It takes 150 pounds (68 kg) of lavender to make just one pound of lavender essential oil. One drop of peppermint essential oil is the equivalent of 142 cups of peppermint tea. Wow, right?

Essential oils are highly concentrated and extremely potent constituents of the plant. They are derived from the volatile oils that the plant produces to ward off insects—a form of natural pesticide. They are unsafe to use directly on skin, and you must use a carrier oil for dilution.

There is some controversy around the use of essential oils, and I recommend that you do your homework and proceed with caution. I use high-quality pure essential oils in very tiny amounts (much less than the recommended amounts) for things such as adding fragrance to a body butter. I do not use them in medicinal remedies such as salves and topical sprays. I never ingest them. At some point, I may forgo my limited use altogether, especially because I have environmental concerns about overharvesting. Always pay attention to any safety information provided and act with caution.

Aromatic Plants

Aromatics such as lavender, mint, basil, rosemary, sage, mugwort, rose, and yarrow possess strong volatile oils. Use them with care, especially when taken internally. Do not brew a tea with an aromatic herb for more than 15 minutes. Also, do not consume them in excess.

Cautions for Herbs in this Book

LAVENDER: Do not consume in excess, as it may cause headache, constipation, or increased appetite. Lavender sometimes causes skin irritation, though this reaction is uncommon, so do a patch-test before full-coverage use. Lavender can interfere with antihypertensive and sedative medications. It should not be consumed prior to surgery. Lavender is possibly unsafe for boys who have not reached puberty, as it can disrupt hormones. There is not enough research available around the use of this herb during pregnancy and breast-feeding, so be safe and avoid its use.

MINT: Do not consume in excess, as it can irritate mucous membranes, the stomach, and skin and cause headaches and heartburn. Some people have skin sensitivity when it comes to mint, so do a patch test before full-coverage use. For pregnant and breast-feeding women, mint is likely safe if consumed in amounts normally found in food but best avoided if taken in a concentrated form like a tincture. The use of concentrated peppermint can interfere with medications that are broken down by the liver and drugs that decrease stomach acid.

BASIL: The use of concentrated basil taken in medicinal amounts can cause low blood sugar or low blood pressure and make bleeding disorders worse. Medicinal amounts are possibly unsafe for pregnant and breast-feeding mothers, risky for people on antihypertensive drugs, and should be avoided before surgery. **Note:** Holy basil (tulsi) is not the same as the kitchen basil in this book, so please do your research if you plan to use it; it has quite a bit of cautions associated with it.

ROSEMARY: Avoid ingestion of large amounts, as it can cause stomach and intestinal irritation, kidney damage, seizures, toxicity, vomiting, excess fluid in the lungs, coma, or miscarriage (so avoid use in pregnancy). Rosemary may cause skin irritation. It may be unsafe for breast-feeding mothers.

SAGE: Some species of sage contain thujone, which can be poisonous if you consume too much. This chemical can cause seizures and damage to the liver and nervous system. Avoid medicinal amounts during pregnancy and breast-feeding, if you have a hormone-sensitive condition, or if you have hypertension issues. Avoid before surgery. Drug interactions with antidiabetic drugs, anticonvulsants, and sedative medications are possible.

DANDELION: There is not enough research on taking medicinal amounts while pregnant or breast-feeding, so avoid use. People with eczema are more prone to having an allergic skin reaction to dandelion. Avoid if you have bleeding disorders, kidney issues, or a ragweed allergy. Dandelion may decrease the effectiveness of antibiotics and has drug interactions with lithium, medications changed by the liver, and potassium-sparing water pills.

BROADLEAF PLANTAIN: Avoid consuming in excess and medicinal amounts if pregnant, as it may increase the chance of miscarriage. It may be unsafe for breast-feeding mothers. Broadleaf plantain can interfere with Warfarin.

MUGWORT: Do not ingest mugwort in large amounts or take it regularly over a long period of time, as excessive quantities can cause damage to the nervous system. Do not use mugwort if pregnant as it can cause contracting of the uterus. It may not be safe for use while breast-feeding. Mugwort may cause allergic reactions in people who have known allergies to the Asteraceae plant family and plants in the Artemisia genus. Some people with sensitive skin find mugwort to be irritating.

CLOVER (RED AND WHITE): Make sure to only use true clover of the Trifolium genus. It is important to use either fully fresh or fully dried blossoms. Avoid browning blossoms, as they contain a harmful cyanide precursor. Red clover, in particular, raises safety concerns when taken medicinally; it contains phytoestrogens that might act like estrogen, so if you have a condition that could be made worse by more estrogen, it is best avoided. Medicinal use is likely unsafe for pregnant and breast-feeding women, as it may cause hormone disruption. Also avoid clover if you have bleeding disorders or Protein S deficiency or if you are to have surgery. Use can also cause rash, headache, muscle ache, nausea, and vaginal bleeding (spotting). Red clover should not be used in combination with certain drugs, including birth control pills, estrogen pills, medications that are broken down and changed by the liver, drugs that slow blood clotting, and Tamoxifen. Be aware that some people have allergic reactions to clover (both red and white), so only try a small amount at first. Some people experience skin sensitivity to red clover, so do a patch test before fully applying a topical preparation.

ROSE: Some people have an allergic reaction to rose petals. Research shows that rose hips (when used in large or medicinal amounts) can have side effects such as fatigue, headache, insomnia, and digestive issues. Large amounts of the vitamin C in rose hip may be unsafe for pregnant or breast-feeding mothers. Rose hip can also increase the chance of kidney stones, heart attack, blood clots, or stroke. Use rose hip with caution if you have an iron deficiency, as it can worsen your condition. Be cautious with rose hip if you take antacids, aspirin, estrogen pill, fluphenazine, lithium, Warfarin, Choline Magnesium Trisalicylate, or Salsalate.

YARROW: Yarrow is toxic to pets. In humans, yarrow sometimes causes skin irritation, so do a patch test first. It is likely unsafe for oral use in pregnancy and should be avoided if you have a bleeding disorder. Yarrow may cause an allergic reaction in those who are sensitive to the Asteraceae family. It should not be consumed in excess, as that can tax the liver and increase photosensitivity. Yarrow contains salicylic acid, so if you are allergic to aspirin you should avoid consuming it. Avoid use if having surgery. Yarrow should not be taken in combination with drugs that slow blood clotting, lithium, sedative medications, antacids, or medications that decrease stomach acids.

PINE: All species of pine have edible parts, but be certain you can positively identify them before use, as some other evergreens are poisonous. Research which types of pine are available in your region. There is not enough reliable information on the safety of pine if you are pregnant or breast-feeding, so be safe and avoid use.

APPLE: No side effects are generally known, other than the danger of cyanide in the seeds, that if eaten in excess can cause death.

Disclaimer

This book is an educational resource. The information in this book is not medical advice and is not a substitute for working with a health care practitioner. If you have a medical condition, take medications, are pregnant or breast-feeding, or otherwise need medical or herbal advice, consult your qualified health care practitioner before using the plants in this book.

There are some references made to plant safety information throughout the book, but it is impossible to address every possible precaution. If a plant in this publication is new to you, consume only a small amount at first if it is edible to see how your body reacts. Do a patch test for a topical preparation before full application. The author and publisher assume no responsibility for adverse reactions or sensitivities to ingredients.

Although the plants used in this book are safe plant allies found in grocery stores, gardens, and, in some cases, are found readily in the wild, you are responsible for educating yourself about plant safety and making sure that you have correctly identified any wild food before picking it, using it topically, or ingesting it.

PART I

....

Witchcraft and the Green Witch's Path

Witches come from all walks of life, and you probably wouldn't know if you passed one on the street. The witch community is diverse, and we honor and celebrate diversity. Witches also have much in common: We have a deep connection to the natural world and a desire to serve the greater good, working with magick through spellcasting and rituals.

We'll begin with an overview of witchcraft basics, sample a variety of spiritual paths that witches take, and examine the evolution of witchcraft. This survey of the Craft provides an important context for better understanding and appreciating the green witch's path. Next, we take a close look at the path of the green witch, which you may have guessed is largely a nature-based form of witchcraft. We'll talk about what it means to identify as a modern green witch and explore the types of spiritual practices that many green witches share.

CHAPTER 1

Witchcraft

Witch. How does that word land for you? No two people I pose this question to have ever responded in exactly the same way. It's such a charged and loaded word, layered with positive and negative connotations. And it's such a personal word—one that individuals define differently for themselves, through meaning that comes from within as opposed to being imposed from without.

Most contemporary witches can agree that a witch is a person who practices witchcraft (commonly called The Craft). We exercise our set of skills to make something using invested energy, intention, artistry, and soul. To fully appreciate the path of the green witch (or any witch's path), we begin by viewing it in relation to witchcraft as a whole: We cannot separate one from the other. This chapter will help you to understand important aspects of green witchcraft from within that greater context. And if you're new to green witchcraft and forging your own individual path, it will give you a better understanding of the choices you have.

Becoming a Witch

My adult life as a green witch has roots in my childhood. I grew up in rural New Jersey in the 1970s and '80s and, ever since I was a little girl, the concept of "witch" has appealed to me. In looking back, I can now recognize the seeds of my Craft that were being planted.

Halloween was and still is my favorite holiday. I remember eschewing the sparkly pink and sugary-sweet princess and angel costumes and instead favoring dressing up as a—you guessed it—witch. Can you relate? I liked the way the dark, flowing costume made me feel inside—all magickal, strong, and special. I did not have the words to adequately express it at the time, but being a witch made me feel present in both the earthly world of the living and the spirit plane.

I have a distinct memory of being eight and sitting by myself on the front porch before going trick-or-treating. I was adorned in black flowing garb and pointy hat, the bittersweet smell of fallen decaying leaves about my feet, a twiggy broom resting in my little lap. A big round moon showed through a cluster of naked trees, high above the mountain. As I gazed at it, I could see myself silhouetted against its glow, flying on my witch's broom.

These visions were not uncommon for me in my youth, as I often had dreams of flying on a broom crafted from the perfect large stick I foraged from the woods. Interestingly, as an adult I craft brooms from carefully selected branches, roots, and twigs I find on the forest floor outside my door, and I use them in my practice of witchcraft. And I do fly! More on that later.

A lot of what I do as a green witch through foraging, gardening, herbalism, and magick has roots in my youth. I recall spending a lot of alone time as a child playing and exploring in the woods, studying and gathering twigs, bark, plants, leaves, nuts, and mushrooms. I played in a naturally occurring fort where I used what I had gathered to concoct pretend potions and brews in an old, black witchy cauldron I found in an historic "garbage dump" on our property—a spot where people from as early as the 1800s left their refuse and unwanted items. On one of my traipses through the woods, I came upon a big chunk of rose quartz crystal lying in fallen leaves. How it got there I have no idea, but I knew it was meant as a present especially for me. Reflecting upon that memory now, I view it as a gift of unconditional love from nature and the world of Spirit, and a validation of where I am at now on my journey as a witch.

As a child, I kept these discoveries and feelings to myself. In hindsight, this was a very good thing as my silence kept these experiences and their outgrowths protected, sacred, untouched, and unharmed by societal misconceptions of what it means to be a witch. I'm not a silent person by nature (in fact, quite the opposite). So perhaps I received a little divine intervention then to help me begin the lifelong journey of being a green witch and to ensure that I'd stay the path. I'm grateful for the protection and guidance, as it allowed me to blossom into the witch I was meant to be.

This childhood inception rings true for so many witches, although there are most certainly powerful witches who did not have this type of early experience.

Falsehoods and Stereotypes Witches Are Up Against

It's common practice for respected dictionaries to define witches as ugly, unpleasant, frightening, overbearing hags with magickal powers, especially evil powers, who practice black witchcraft with the help of the devil. These stereotypical misconceptions, which persist to this day, were born of the patriarchy, specifically of the Church, as early as 392 CE, when Christian leaders forced pagan people to turn away from the beauty and magick of the natural world.

This set the stage across Europe and North America for centuries of persecution of countless natural healers, herbalists, and midwives—the ancestors of green witches. These innocent people, most of whom were women who, instead of being valued and revered for their natural gifts they used in service to others, were stripped of their personal power and accused of being evil witches who should be exterminated.

If you do an image search for the word *witch*, you will find it limited to mostly two kinds of stereotypes, directed at women. One, the old, scary woman with bulging demonic eyes, long warty nose, and bony fingers poised to cast an evil spell on you, like the green-skinned Wicked Witch of the West. Or two, appearing less frequently, but still as an obvious stereotype, is a symbol of temptation embodied by the young, sexy, alluring female witch dressed to kill in a tight, black dress and high heels. Not that I have anything against wearing that attire, but I am definitely against stereotypes and the objectification of women. I love the charming comedy *Hocus Pocus* and the Sanderson sisters of Salem, but I think it's important to recognize how they are stereotypically portrayed as child-eating, nasty, ugly, and sexy lone spinsters.

Finding Your Path

Take a moment to pause and think about personal experiences you may have had in years past that have pointed you toward your becoming as a witch. What set you on your path? Or, perhaps you are now being called to begin. What validations have you received? These experiences need not be grand or earth-shattering. There is magick to be found in the mundane.

What Does It Really Mean to Be a Witch?

A witch identifies as a witch. A witch is in touch with nature and their own personal power, in whatever form that takes—through herbalism, activism, energy work, or psychic work—the possibilities for service are endless. Witches practice magick through things such as spellwork, rituals, divination, incantations, and prayer, all based on ancient practices that were around long before Christianity. In fact, Christianity co-opted many of these practices and based their holidays on the pagan holidays.

Magick is not this lofty, unattainable, supernatural thing. It's pretty down to earth actually, especially for the green witch. It involves getting in touch with one's personal power. It's about working in concert with nature and the Universe to raise, harness, and direct energies to produce positive change. That's it in a nutshell. I'd like to believe that every human being is interested in that kind of work, on some level, whether or not they identify as a witch.

Taking Back Our Power and Walking Our Own Path

I love the word *witch*. For me, there's something delicious and empowering about saying it and hearing it. Yes, it's associated with incorrect and damaging slander that has been used for centuries to defile the feminine archetypes, vilify natural healers, and ultimately disempower women. But just like with other similar brutal derogatory terms, the targeted people eventually wish to empower themselves by "taking the word back," and that's why so many women, some men, nonbinary and trans people are now reclaiming and redefining the word *witch*. Taking it back is key for healing the extreme damage done to our ancestors and for replacing the pain and suffering with the true meaning of what it means to be a witch. It allows us to rise up once again, especially now, when our gifts are sorely needed.

I don't follow a traditional, initiatory path. I'm predominantly a green witch with strong hedge witch inclinations. I'm not Wiccan, and I don't consider myself to be pagan. I don't worship the goddess and god deities that fall into that framework, although I draw inspiration from them. I celebrate sabbats, and I am drawn to the power of the moon. I don't belong to a coven, as I prefer being a solo practitioner. A mouthful, right?

It's refreshing and exciting to see that there are many ways to be a witch. You have freedom when it comes to defining and forging your path as a witch. As you think about your interest in green witchcraft, I want this book to help you make choices that are a good fit for you and to forge a feeling of connection with you.

Identifying as a green witch comes naturally to me, and I think that's because I've spent an abundance of my life out in the woods, connecting to and attuning myself with the natural world. There's magick *everywhere* out there. The sacred is all around, in the elements of Earth, Air, Fire, Water, and Spirit. Achieving harmony with nature and its cycles has given my life meaning, purpose, a sense of peace, and the ability to recognize energy magick in simple, everyday occurrences.

I am a folk herbalist, avid forager, and gardener, which are all earthy green witch associations. I also feel a strong connection to the Spirit World, and I practice divination in many forms, including tarot reading and scrying, which are more associated with hedge witchery. I practice energy arts such as Reiki and using crystals.

For me, identifying as a witch also means being comfortable in my own skin and exercising my gifts and powers, not only in fostering healing through herbalism and energy arts but also as an activist, artist, and teacher. Calling myself a witch feels good and right. I have realized that I've been a witch all along, in this life and probably in past ones, and in my forties I came out of the broom closet and claimed myself as one. It feels tremendously healing.

Commonalities among Witches

There are more similarities among witches than there are differences. Below is a list of common beliefs and practices that many witches share. I relate to them all, to varying degrees.

A CONNECTION TO NATURE. Witches recognize that energy exists in all things, from plants and animals to minerals and geographic formations. We have reverence for and a sense of responsibility toward the environment.

SERVICE TO OTHERS. Many witches seek out roles to heal, assist, and teach others.

A BELIEF IN NON-ABSOLUTES. We believe in abstract, non-dualistic thinking—that there are no absolutes (i.e., dark versus light, good versus evil).

THE PRACTICE OF MAGICK. There is debate around what magick actually is, but for this book it means *working with natural forces to bring about transformation.* This comes naturally to the green witch. Spellwork is used to create change or transformation. Witches also practice divination to gain insight by tapping into the Higher Self,

our intuition, the Collective Unconscious, and the Spirit World of gods, goddesses, guides, and ancestors. Divination can be useful in informing and guiding our spellwork.

THE PERFORMANCE OF RITUALS. Witches may conduct rituals for various reasons, including honoring a deity, marking a sabbat, or celebrating a full moon.

A SACRED SPACE. Witches create a space to practice their craft. This could be a room, a corner in your home, or even a mobile altar. I have a dedicated "witch room," as we call it in my house, that serves as an apothecary and contains multiple altars.

OBSERVANCE OF THE WHEEL OF THE YEAR. The witch's calendar is marked by sabbats such as Samhain, Yule, and Beltane. Observance of the sabbats varies among witches.

Essentials for Your Craft

In our rituals and spellwork, witches typically draw on one or more of the following:

- Elemental magick using Earth, Air, Fire, Water, Spirit, The Four Directions (North, South, East, West)
- Herbs
- Crystals ("bones of the Earth")
- Candles
- Color magick
- "Day of the week" magickal correspondences

Some witches also incorporate astrology and planetary influences (including sun and moon) into their practice.

Distinctions between Witchcraft, Paganism, and Wicca

Paganism is a term used to define the spiritual practices of people before the existence of Christianity. Oxford Dictionary defines paganism as "a religion other than one of the main world religions, specifically a non-Christian or pre-Christian religion." The Pagan Federation describes paganism as any ancient religions based on the religions of Classical Antiquity, primarily in Persia, Egypt, Greece, and Rome. The word is derived from classical Latin and means "rural," "rustic," and "civilian." It was used in the fourth century by early Christians as a derogatory way to label people in the Roman Empire who were not Christian and who worshiped nature. Some of these non-Christians practiced polytheism (the worshiping of multiple deities). A similar term used in this manner is "heathen."

The rituals pagans created eventually became the Wheel of the Year, a neopagan term for the yearly cycle of seasonal holidays (sabbats) observed by many contemporary pagans and witches. It's structured around the year's main solar occurrences (solstices and equinoxes) and the midpoints between them. One could argue that paganism is at the root of witchcraft in general. Twentieth-century modern paganism, often called neopaganism, has roots in older pagan practices and beliefs, specifically from Eastern and Western Europe and countries settled by Europeans.

Wicca is an example of a neopagan religion. It is an initiatory-based, modern pagan religious movement that's founded on pre-Christian traditions and holidays of northern and western Europe. It began in England in the early 1900s and was then formally unveiled to the public in 1954 by British civil servant Gerald Gardner. Doreen Valiente is noted for partnering with Gardner and writing Wiccan scriptural texts. Wiccans typically worship the goddess and god, with emphasis on the goddess. They observe the Wheel of the Year, and many also observe the cycles of the moon. Gardnerian Wicca is the first known modern pagan tradition to go public, but it is not the only type of Wicca.

Not all witches are Wiccan. A Christian witch is not Wiccan or pagan by definition (although they may observe sabbats in addition to Christian holidays, most of which are based on sabbats). Some Wiccans worship deities without practicing witchcraft. There are witches who identify as pagan, while some do not. Others identify as pagan, but not as a witch.

So, what does this all mean when it comes to your practice? For me, as a green witch, having this information makes me more aware, more open, and more respectful of the varying ways that people embody the archetype of witch. It can also help inform our practice and guide us in deciding which resources can best support our practice.

The Explosive Growth of Witchcraft: An Exciting Time to Be a Witch

The witch population has experienced major growth in recent years, and witchcraft is now a popular part of mainstream culture, primarily because of millennials and their approach to spirituality and response to the current political environment. Thank you, millennials! I'm a witch in her late forties, and I greatly appreciate this fresh, young energy. Instead of being taboo, witchcraft and witches are being revered for their intuitive powers and wise ways, at least in parts of the world. There's been a flourish of interest in the subjects of astrology, tarot, and crystals. Look at all the books on witchcraft that are being published. The podcasts. Witch-themed Instagram accounts. It's so inspiring and encouraging!

A Pew Research Center report from 2014 stated that near three-quarters of a million American adults identify as Wiccan or pagan. I suspect that if Pew did the survey again today, the numbers would be much higher. Of course, not all witches are Wiccan or pagan, and not all Wiccans and pagans are witches.

When we look back on the history of witchcraft, specifically in the United States and in Europe, we see clear surges in the interest of witchcraft that correlate with events that stimulate public distrust in authority. The surges are often a response to being oppressed and marginalized by those in charge and involve regaining control and rooting into one's own personal power. This topic is discussed in a March 2020 article in *The Atlantic* that features Juliet Diaz, author of *Witchery*, and Pam Grossman, author of *Waking the Witch* and host of the popular podcast *The Witch Wave*. The article, written by Bianca Bosker, points out correlations between the rise of witchcraft and events and movements such as nineteenth-century feminism and transcendentalism, the second wave of feminism, Woodstock, the Civil Rights movement, the Anita Hill hearings in the 1990s, and again with the 2016 United States presidential election and the rise of the #MeToo movement that followed.

A Brief Sampling of Paths

When it comes to witches, it feels counterintuitive to classify paths; witches are free spirits and don't wish to be put in a box. On the flipside, labels can also empower and help to convey meaning. Remember that the following sampling is not an all-inclusive list by any means, and that varying and sometimes contradictory interpretations exist. For example, there is debate about what traditional witchcraft is. Some consider Wicca to be a traditional path, while practitioners of older paths consider themselves to be traditional and object to classifying Wicca as traditional. It is almost impossible to create a condensed list that accurately reflects every facet of witchcraft, as witchcraft comes in many forms with varying interpretations and is ever-evolving and ever-changing.

Recent Paths

With the explosion of witchcraft and its rooting in mainstream culture, we see new types of paths emerging, such as glam, gray, and sea witches. Although I'm a green witch, I, like others, relate to and am inspired by the practices of my fellow witches who follow different paths.

Glam witches are often devotees of the goddess Lilith and focus their practice of witchcraft on glamour, sex, crystal, and moon magick, using clothing, makeup, color, and scents to manipulate energies and experiences. They are charismatic, shape-shifting geniuses.

Gray witches, often called *neutral witches*, recognize that nothing is ever "black or white" or "good or bad." As practitioners of magick, they work to balance "opposite" forces, finding that middle ground. Their aims are for the greater good, striving for balance and harmony, embracing the reality of both light and dark energies.

Sea witches are like gray witches in that they recognize, through the symbolism of the sea, that nature is both nurturing and destructive. Sea witches generally live near the ocean and draw from its powers to fuel their practice of witchcraft. If you are a green witch who lives by the sea, I believe you'll have a lot in common with the sea witch.

Older Traditional and Folk Witches

This category is broad and includes witches whose traditions have been passed down through generations. The following Old Craft practices embody the old ways before the founding of Wicca:

- Shamanism—often associated with indigenous and tribal societies
- Vodou—African diaspora tradition of Haiti
- Voodoo—Vodou-related pop culture tradition specific to the Caribbean and the southern United States in places such as New Orleans

"Magick" with a "K"

Magick is a common term coined by Aleister Crowley, an English occultist of the nineteenth century, in contrast with "magic," which involves tricks and illusion.

Being a Witch

Take a moment to think about what being a witch looks like for you. Keep in mind that the experience is unique to each witch and that you have the freedom to forge your own path. You are a magickal being who has everything you need already inside to become the witch you were meant to be or, more accurately, to remember the witch within you that you already are.

- Hoodoo—also known as Conjure and Rootwork, and a form of southern American folk magick
- Brujería—present in Latin American and Afro-Caribbean cultures
- Stregheria—has southern European roots and includes Italian American witchcraft

It is important to know that there are issues of cultural appropriation around these traditions as outsiders co-opt, exploit, and misrepresent sacred spiritual practices of indigenous groups to which they do not belong. Witches outside of these cultures need to be mindful of this, so they don't inadvertently appropriate sacred names and practices, and so they can help protect these sacred traditions.

For instance, as a white person, I would never call myself a Bruja, as that word is reserved for witches of Latin American and Afro-Caribbean cultures. Another example is that I have special relationships with a few animals that I consider my guides. I do not call them my "spirit animals" or use the language "animal totem," as those terms

are very specific names for sacred practices of indigenous peoples, and I have no right to claim them. Instead, I talk about animal helpers, soul helpers, and spirit guides.

Appropriated terms are used quite loosely in popular culture, resulting in the commodification and erasure of very specific, holy practices of indigenous peoples who have been colonized and marginalized. Don't beat yourself up if you've made this mistake, as we are all learning. But make some changes and reparations. When we know better, we do better—or at least we should!

Formal Initiatory Neopagan Traditions

These paths are religion-based and include Gardnerian Wicca (and other types of Wicca, such as Alexandrian), Neo-Druidism, and Crowleyan Thelema. This category appeals to witches who prefer a more formal group approach to witchcraft, rites of passage, a body of more fixed beliefs, and, in some traditions, hierarchical structure.

Celebrating Diversity in the Witch Community

Finally, we come to the eclectic witches, which I would argue most witches are, at least to some degree, unless they strictly follow a traditional path. Other terms to know are natural-born or hereditary witch versus self-guided witch. Natural-born/hereditary refers to familial traditional witchcraft that is passed down from generation to generation as opposed to the self-guided witch who forges their own individually defined path. Solitary witches versus witches who are members of a coven are pretty self-explanatory terms. Green, hedge, kitchen/hearth/cottage witches, and newer types such as gray, sea, and glamour witches are typically, but not always, solitary practitioners.

They may also be part of a coven. Witches who belong to more formal groups with a ceremonial approach to witchcraft tend to be members of covens, but they can choose to practice alone.

It may seem like there are an overwhelming amount of ways to describe oneself as a witch, and you may be left wondering if these labels are necessary. I think they are. First, these descriptors demonstrate that there is no one way to be a witch. There are lots of choices, and we are invited to define witchcraft for ourselves and forge a personal path that aligns with our own unique gifts. Second, these descriptors diversify the witch community to the extent that we cannot be pinned down, marginalized, and persecuted quite as easily.

Green Witchcraft

Green witches revere nature and connect with green energy in numerous ways. We are environmentalists, herbalists, naturalists, gardeners, and foragers.

Similar paths, which are often considered to be aspects of green witchcraft, are kitchen and hedge witchcraft. Green, kitchen, and hedge witches generally follow nonreligious, self-guided, solitary paths. Kitchen witches, also known as cottage and hearth witches, are labeled with descriptors that are relatively new to the witch scene but ancient in practice. They focus their Craft on home life, specifically weaving natural magick into everyday domestic actions such as cooking, cleaning, and creating sacred space.

The term *hedge witch* has both literal and figurative meaning. Historically, hedge witches lived in the hedge, or the border separating the forest from the everyday life of the village. Living as a recluse was probably something that was imposed upon them for being different but also chosen by the hedge witch for both privacy reasons and for easy access to the forest and its healing energies and gifts.

Hedge witches are known for planting their feet firmly in both realms—one foot in the earthly realm and the other in the Otherworld, or spirit realm. They are known for practicing divination and spirit communication. They are also known for a special skill known as hedge riding. This is similar to astral projection and allows them to travel to the Otherworld to obtain spiritual guidance and wisdom to use in service to others in the earthly realm. If I labeled myself as a witch for the sake of conveying meaning to you, I'd call myself a "green witch in the hedge."

CHAPTER 2

The Green Witch's Path

Now that we've explored some witchcraft basics and the variety of paths that witches take, we can more fully understand and appreciate the path of the green witch within that greater picture. This chapter takes a look at the green witches who came before us—who they were, the persecution they endured, and the nature-based spiritual practices and beliefs they passed down to us. And we in turn will incorporate their teachings into our lives, reverently working with plants and green energy in whatever way feels authentic to us. We will pass down the knowledge and what we have learned from nature, our greatest teacher, all with the same aim as green witches of the past—to bring about balance, harmony, and healing.

The Roots of Green Witchcraft

Green witchcraft comes from the oldest of traditions, grounded in the powers of nature. Hereditary witch Ann Moura calls it the Green Craft, which echoes a time before the development of hierarchical religions, lawmakers, and the warrior class. The roots of this path are strongly pragmatic and linked to survival in times when people filled various roles in their community—jobs such as hunter, gatherer, cook, builder, craftsperson, and healer.

The original green witches were the folk healers and practitioners of folk magick. They were the herbalists, midwives, caregivers, and death doulas. The original green witches, like the hedge witches, lived on the fringes of their communities, both literally and figuratively. Yes, they were treated as outcasts—but some probably also wished to be left alone and liked living near nature and its resources, making it easier to partner with Mother Earth to do their life's work.

A History of Persecution

The roots and evolved path of the green witch, or any witch, are tied to the grim centuries of persecution that our ancestors of witchcraft endured. The best-known recorded information on the subject is confined to European and North American history, from the late Middle Ages spanning through the witch hunts and Burning Times (1450–1750 CE), including the Salem witch trials. The following are some important dates and events—by no means a comprehensive list!

- The idea of women as being inferior to men begins in ancient Greek and Roman times, setting the stage for centuries of persecution at the hands of the Church and patriarchal society.

- During the twelfth and thirteenth centuries, a series of Inquisitions lead to the torture and execution of non-Christians.

- In 1275 CE, Angéle de la Barthe of Toulouse, France is sentenced by an Inquisitor and burned to death for "practicing witchcraft."

- Historians estimate that from approximately 1450 to 1750 CE, 40,000 to 100,000 people (mostly women, and mostly non-witches) were executed for "practicing witchcraft," although the numbers are probably much higher, as not all executions were recorded properly, if at all.

- Heinrich Kramer's dark, deathly *Malleus Maleficarum (Hammer of Witches)*, a guide to finding and torturing witches, is published in 1486 CE.

- More than 200 women and men are accused of witchcraft in Salem, Massachusetts, from 1692 to 1693 CE. Fourteen women and five men are executed. In Salem, and throughout Europe, it is believed that many of these accusations and executions were attempts at ruthless land grabs. In a lesser-known witch hunt in Hartford, Connecticut, from 1661 to 1663, more than a dozen people are accused of witchcraft and three women and a man are hung.

- In the early to mid-nineteenth century, the Spiritualism movement takes off in North America and Europe, starting in upstate New York. This movement, especially enjoyed by middle- and upper-class women, involves communication with the dead via seances and psychic mediums, which makes being a psychic medium or witch more socially acceptable. This sets the tone for future endeavors such as the popularity of psychic mediums and the creation of Wicca, followed by the rise of self-guided witchcraft, of which green witchcraft is a part.

- In 1951 CE, England dismisses its law that allowed for the imprisonment of accused witches. British civil servant Gerald Gardner (and Doreen Valiente) unveil and establish Wicca.

The brutal persecution of witches occurred worldwide historically and still happens today in many places. There have been recorded incidences of oppression in China, Saudi Arabia, Indonesia, Nigeria, and Papua New Guinea. Saudi Arabia has a special police unit that "scientifically" hunts for witches, and the punishment for the practice of witchcraft is beheading. In 2017, the United Nations held its first meeting to discuss witchcraft-related violence.

Identifying as a Modern Green Witch

The path of the modern green witch is an individual, earth-honoring, informal one that emphasizes independence, freedom, and a strong sense of self. It's a very flexible path— more a mindset and an approach to witchcraft than a fixed way of practicing. Today's green witches come from all walks of life and live in cities, towns, and rural areas (being in the country can make practicing green witchcraft easier in a lot of ways).

While all witches connect with and revere nature, green witches do so by working with plants and green energy. They are contemporary naturalists, botanists, herbalists, foragers, wildcrafters, gardeners, environmentalists, and eco-friendly individuals seeking to live in a way that minimizes harm to the environment. Their deep reverence for and sensitivity to the Earth and Her limited resources is what makes a green witch wish to protect the planet, our home, and all Her inhabitants—plant, animal, and mineral.

Spiritual Practices

A green witch generally forges a nonreligious, spiritual path that values and honors the natural world. But a green witch may also be a religious person. For example, they may also be Wiccan or they may be Christian, but paramount in their belief system is recognizing the Divine in nature and seeing themselves as a part of this divine tapestry of life. They commit to use their gifts to serve, honor, and protect our planet and all its life forms.

The opportunity to walk this personal path requires nothing more than initiation from a green witch's own heart—not the permission or blessing of an outside entity or force. There is no set doctrine or tenets to follow. No required rituals or holidays, although many witches, myself included, celebrate the Wheel of the Year (page 33).

Green witches do not usually worship goddesses and gods, as seen in neopagan religions such as Wicca, but they may look to them for inspiration. These human-made deities, each associated with a particular aspect of the Divine, have accumulated vast amounts of collective energy over the centuries from the people who connect with them—strong energy and an ancient power that can be tapped into and used to fuel one's magickal practices.

Finding Inspiration

Although I don't practice polytheism, I identify with the energies of several goddesses and draw inspiration, knowledge, and wisdom from them. A particular deity may catch your attention and call to you, or you may identify with deities with qualities and mythic stories that can guide you on your own personal journey. I tend to identify with goddess figures who are androgynous and embody both fiery masculine energy and softer, nurturing feminine energy, and deities with witchy and nature-based bents. For example, I have an affinity for the Greek goddess Artemis who is accompanied by a deer—the goddess of the forests and the hills, the wild animals, and the hunt. Also, I relate to the energy of Hecate, Greek Goddess of magick, witchcraft, necromancy (which involves communicating with the dead and divination practices), and herbology regarding both healing and poisonous plants.

I am fascinated by The Morrígan, an evocative, androgynous Celtic goddess who is often described as a trio of sisters called "the three Morrígna." This triple goddess figure is associated with war and fertility—birth and death—the cycle of life. Also known as the Phantom Queen and shape-shifter, The Morrígan is all about transformation and is perfect for calling upon for aid in shadow work, where we face and reflect on the hidden, darker parts of ourselves that require acknowledgment and healing.

Also calling to me is Lilith, a figure from Jewish mythology who was born of the same clay as Adam but refused to become subservient to him and was kicked out of the Garden of Eden. In Gardnerian Wicca, Lilith is associated with the priestess of the coven. Doreen Valiente, who wrote the bulk of religious liturgy within the Gardnerian tradition, called Lilith the presiding goddess of The Craft. There are many misconceptions and stereotypes of Lilith out there, but I believe that she embodies the witch archetype.

The Wheel of the Year: 8 Pagan Sabbats

The Wheel of the Year is made up of religious festivals (called sabbats) of the neopaganism movement based on folk traditions. They are marked by the winter and summer solstices, the equinoxes (called quarters), and the holidays that fall in between them (called cross-quarter days). See illustration on page 33. Observing them is a natural way for green witches to deeply connect with and honor the Earth through Her changing seasons and tap into and continue to feed the collective energies of people who have made these same observances for thousands of years.

Samhain
(October 31 through November 1)

This sabbat, the witch's New Year, coincides with Halloween. Samhain celebrates the final harvest of the year and invites us to enjoy the fruits of our labors, reflect on the year, and set goals and intentions for the new year ahead. The veil between the earthly realm and the Spirit World is said to be at its thinnest this time of year, making it an ideal time for spirit communication and honoring our deceased loved ones.

Yule
(Winter Solstice, December 20–23)

This holiday marks the longest night of the year and the beginning of a waxing period when the amount of sunlight increases daily, inviting us to celebrate the return of light and embrace renewal, hope, and creativity. Yule is a time to rest (likened to hibernating in winter), go inward, and engage in what is known as shadow work, reflecting on the parts of ourselves that need attention and healing.

Imbolc
(February 1)

Imbolc, the first cross-quarter holiday of the year, falls halfway between the Winter Solstice and the Spring Equinox. As we head toward spring, we recognize the signs of Mother Earth waking up again. This holiday recognizes and celebrates Brigid, the Celtic goddess who watches over and protects one's home, hearth, and farm.

Ostara
(Spring Equinox, March 20–22)

Ostara heralds the first day of spring, when the length of day and night are equal. It's named after the ancient Anglo-Saxon goddess of spring and the dawn. This is a fertile time to plant seeds, both literally in the earth and figuratively in one's life. Begin again, create, and move forward with balance and vibrance.

Beltane
(April 30 through May 1)

This is the second cross-quarter day of the year, landing between the Spring Equinox and the Summer Solstice and coinciding with May Day. We celebrate the return of full sun, the element of Fire, sensuality, and passion. Traditionally, bonfires are lit on Beltane to represent the power of the sun this time of year.

Litha
(Summer Solstice, June 20–23)

Litha marks the Summer Solstice, the longest day of the year with the shortest night. We celebrate the sun at its height, followed by a slow descent—a waning period where the amount of sunlight and energy decreases daily.

Lammas Day or Lughnasadh
(August 1)

This cross-quarter day embarks on the harvest season and is the first of three harvest celebrations, the other two being Mabon and Samhain. It's named after Lugh, the Celtic sun deity, and is traditionally celebrated with feasting, merriment, and singing.

Mabon
(Autumn Equinox, September 20–23)

Mabon falls on the Autumn Equinox, the first day of fall, and is the second harvest celebration. Night and day are perfectly balanced, with equal amounts of light. At Mabon, we observe the cycle of life in nature, of which death is a part, and of which we are a part. We show gratitude for the abundance of the harvest and embrace our descent into the darker colder months, knowing that rebirth will occur once more come spring.

Yule

WINTER SOLSTICE

Samhain

Imbolc

NEW YEAR

BRIGID'S DAY

SPRING EQUINOX

AUTUMN EQUINOX

Mabon

Ostara

MAY DAY

LAMMAS DAY

Beltane

Lughnasadh

SUMMER SOLSTICE

Litha

Other Green Magickal Practices

Green witches enrich their path with some or all of the following nature-based practices. Other types of witches certainly engage in these practices too, but the green witch is intrinsically attracted to them, as they provide direct connection to the magickal gifts of nature.

Elemental Magick

Drawing on the elements to boost the power of spellwork and divination practices. Earth. Air. Fire. Water. Spirit. They are the essential elements of the natural world that the green witch lives in and works with. In fact, each herb is associated with one of the elements, which define the energy of the plant and help to inform the green witch of its magickal uses.

Animism

A word derived from the Latin *anima*, which means "breath, spirit, life." It is the belief that all things—plants, animals, minerals, trees, geographic features, weather, and perhaps even handmade objects—are imbued with spiritual essence.

Use of Herbs

Green witches work with the natural vibrations of plants for both medicinal and magickal purposes, which are actually closely linked. In this book, we will be sticking with simple, safe plant allies (many available at the grocery store or grown in your gardens) and co-creating with them to make a variety of homemade remedies and magickal applications for spells and divination. Sorry, no work with mandrake root or belladonna blooms in this book.

Crystal Work

Crystals, often called "bones of the Earth," are as old as the Earth, and are alive in the sense that they are filled with energy and act as conduits of energy. These gifts of the Earth are often utilized by green witches in their spellwork, rituals, and divination practices. They're used to raise one's own energy, amplify the energy of one's spells, and for healing. Crystals are often used in conjunction with herbs such as adding them to herbal anointing oils, placing them in a garden or potted plant to promote life or as an offering, incorporating them in spell jars with herbs, and more.

Honoring the Sun and Moon

Planet Earth is part of the greater galaxy that shares the energies of the sun and moon. The sun provides life and energy to the Earth and all its inhabitants, while the moon controls the tides and thus the availability of water to the roots of plants. The

The Call of Plants

Have you ever had a particular medicinal plant call to you, perhaps growing outside your door, or repeatedly popping up in your life? That plant wishes to work with you and is picking up on the vibrations you are sending out for it, often in an unconscious way. Or maybe you love hugging trees and have a favorite one you communicate with. Do you have a special relationship with an animal helper? Those are all examples of animism—a concept that is naturally embraced by the green witch.

celebration of the eight sabbats of the Wheel of the Year (page 33) focuses on the cycles of the sun.

Green witches often partake in full moon celebrations that involve the channeling of the moon's energies for boosting the power of one's spellwork and divination practices. Some also celebrate other phases of the moon, such as the Dark Moon (also known as the New Moon and the Crone Moon), and the Crescent Moon, representing the lunar phase in its first quarter—an opportune time for setting goals and intentions, and starting new ventures.

All plants have planetary associations, of which the sun and moon are a part. Sun plants are associated with healing, protection, and legal matters, while moon plants correspond with peace, healing, sleep, prophetic dreams, and fertility. Examples of sun plants include chamomile, cinnamon, rosemary, St. John's wort, and witch hazel. Examples of moon plants include lemon balm, jasmine, lily, poppy, and wintergreen.

Building Natural Altars

Witches create altars that serve a variety of purposes. They can be used as a space for things such as spellwork and rituals. They can be used for expressing devotion for a deity or an entity such as the moon or as a way to embrace or counteract the effects of an astrological event such as "Mercury in retrograde." Natural altars are also a convenient space for divination practices such as scrying (page 154), as a shrine in honor of one's ancestors, or to work with the elements, the Four Directions, or with concepts such as love, healing, protection, abundance, or fertility.

Fostering Balance and Teaching Others

Green witches honor the Divine in nature and recognize that they themselves are part of the tapestry of the Earth that is made up of all living things: Everything is interconnected. Green witches view magick as a natural, everyday occurrence rather than something separate from their way of life. This makes it easy for green witches to tap into the natural vibrations of Earth's green energy and work with it in medicinal and magickal ways. They dedicate their lives to helping bring back balance to the natural world. Herbalism, for instance, is all about creating remedies that heal an imbalance in the body. Herbalist green witches, like myself, co-create with plants to make safe, simple, healing remedies for self, family, loved ones, and community.

Green witches consider the natural world to be a teacher. They take in nature and its lessons through their senses by listening, watching, touching, smelling, and sometimes tasting and then work with green energy to bring about balance, harmony, and healing. Green witches align themselves with the "wise woman" tradition of healing,

Found Treasures

Green witches naturally incorporate objects from nature into their altars. I like to include natural objects I find in the forests, fields, and rocky coast of Maine where I live. My treasures include objects such as flora I forage or grow in my garden, wildcrafted wands and besoms (a witch's broom) made from twigs and branches I find on the forest floor, dried mushrooms, shells, animal bones, stones and crystals, feathers, a bottle of storm water, herbal bundles for smoke cleansing, and pressed autumn leaves from my annual October trip to Salem, Massachusetts. In the warmer months, I enjoy building altars outdoors in the woods on top of moss-covered stumps.

co-creating with plant allies to make remedies for healing of self and healing of others. Green witches honor a calling to share what they've been taught, to pass on a forgotten knowledge— a knowledge that is each person's birthright.

This knowledge has important implications for the state of the modern world; it helps others reconnect to nature and planet Earth and to become sensitive to the fact that Her precious resources are limited, which spurs on wanting to protect Her, to heal our broken relationship with the environment, and to restore balance. It's a reciprocal relationship, where if we respect, revere, and honor the Earth and take responsibility for Her, we provide Her with health. She in turn will do the same for us.

PART II

·················

13 Essential Plant Allies for the
Green Witch's Cupboard

I'm excited to introduce you to the thirteen essential plants for the witch's cupboard—safe, healing plant allies we can work with for medicinal, culinary, and magickal purposes. I carefully selected wild plants that grow readily throughout the world and plants that can be easily cultivated in our gardens, grown in a sunny window, or purchased from a local market. I've also included plants that are considered both wild and cultivated, such as the rose. I wanted to make sure that all readers have easy and safe access to plants in this book, so some choices are practical but no less beneficial and powerful.

Be sure to do your research to ensure safest use of these plants. Also remember that even though there are traditional magickal associations and correspondences given for each plant, what matters most is how you relate to the spiritual energy of the plants and how they speak to you individually.

It's time to meet the plants and form a connection and relationship with each one as you become intimately familiar with them. I am willing to bet you will fall in love with them—with their spirits.

CHAPTER 3

Meet the Plants

Kitchen Garden Herbs

K itchen garden herbs are cultivated plants (known as *cultivars*), which means they are planted and cared for. Some cultivated plants can become naturalized in a region: Once they are planted, they establish themselves and spread with ease all on their own, without further care.

The kitchen garden herbs in this chapter—lavender, mint, basil, rosemary, and sage—are all a part of the Lamiaceae family (also known as the mint family). This family contains 236 genera and more than 7,000 species, available worldwide. Its aromatic plants are valued for their delicious flavors and enchanting fragrances and for their potent natural medicine and their magick. They are readily available, easy-to-grow, hardy plants and will provide you with a valuable, powerful resource for your herbal home remedies and magickal workings.

Lavender (*Lavandula angustifolia*)

FOLK NAMES: English Lavender, Common Lavender, True Lavender, Elf Leaf, Nardus, Nard

FAMILY: Lamiaceae

ASTROLOGY: Mercury, Gemini, Virgo

ELEMENT: Air

PLANT LORE: The delightful smell of lavender has the power to transport you to another time and place. Lavender comes from the Latin word *lavare*, which means "to wash." Lavender was used by ancient Greeks and Romans to sweeten their soaps, perfumes, bathwater, and laundry. In the fourteenth century, lavender was worn to ward off the Black Plague in Europe—and it helped, as it repelled the fleas that caused the plague. In Victorian times, lavender was used as an aromatic spirit to counter a fainting spell.

MAGICKAL CORRESPONDENCES: love, protection, purification, cleansing negative energies, peace, sleep, dreams, longevity, happiness, balance, healing, friendship, communication, travel, divination, psychic powers, intellect, wisdom

Identification

There are thirty-nine species of lavender and more than 400 varieties. The most common type is English Lavender, which, ironically, is native to the Mediterranean, not England. It forms small, tubular blossoms (known as *inflorescences*) on its silvery-green, narrow-leafed stalks, which come in various cultivated colors such as lavender, violet-blue, blue-purple, and white-pink.

Lavender is aromatic when rubbed or crushed and smells clean, fresh, floral, and sweet, with a note of camphor that's pungent and has a slightly bitter taste. This herb grows 2 to 3 feet tall (60 to 90 cm), and it has a blooming period of early summer through late summer. It prefers full sun and sandy, well-drained soil, and is considered a perennial herb in zones 5 to 9.

PARTS USED: aerial parts, generally the flower buds

Medicinal and Culinary Uses

Lavender is well known for reducing anxiety, lifting one's mood, instilling a sense of calm, and relaxing the body, mind, and soul. Lavender repairs skin damaged by small cuts, sunburn, minor burns, and eczema. It pairs well with broadleaf plantain and dandelion for healing skin. Its analgesic qualities will ease joint and muscle pain and encourage circulation, aiding in the healing process. Lavender also boosts the appetite, and it's deliciously soothing as a culinary herb.

- Sip a cup of lavender bud tea or add some to a tea blend. Use 1 heaping teaspoon of dried herb per 1 cup (235 ml) of boiling water, allowing it to steep 10 to 15 minutes.

- Make lavender glycerite, a glycerin-based tincture for medicinal purposes (page 130).

- Place blossoms in your pillow (or in an eye pillow) to promote a restful sleep.

- Add lavender to a simmering potpourri (page 177).

- Make a perfume by blending lavender with other essential oils in a carrier oil.

- Soothe a headache by applying lavender oil at the temples. Create an infused oil (page 131) or use it in essential oil form diluted with a carrier oil.

- Treat acne with a face wash made from a strong lavender tea. You can make a lavender-infused topical spray with a blend of lavender tincture (made with lavender blossoms) and distilled water. Make it in the same way you would make the Yarrow Clear-Skin Topical Spray (page 145).

- Create a lavender salve (page 138, variation). Rub it into skin to act as a bug repellent. It also treats insect bites, bee stings, poison ivy, and the rash from stinging nettle. If you need it in a pinch for bites, stings, or rashes, create a paste with lavender, baking soda, and water. A tea-soaked cloth compress also works.

- Tuck a lavender sachet into wool sweaters to repel moths.

- Include lavender in a household cleaning spray (page 181), as it has disinfectant properties and is an effective herb for killing lice.

- Add a handful of lavender blossoms to bath water (or place in a small muslin bag first) to relax and lift your mood and ease tired muscles and achy joints. It also makes an excellent foot bath for reviving tired feet.

- Infuse blossoms in honey (page 123, variation), lemonade, wines, and vinegars.

- Incorporate lavender into baked goods and puddings, or make candy, lavender sugar, or jelly. Make a lavender simple syrup for cocktails or to pour over ice cream. Sprinkle lavender on fruit salad. Make lavender-infused cream for a dessert coffee.

Magickal Uses

Lavender is a powerful herb for spiritual work, as it brings you into a necessary relaxed state, puts you in touch with high vibrations, and encourages clear thinking. Lavender can be used to cleanse negative energies and protect you from them. Historically, people have tossed lavender into their summer bonfires to ensure a good year.

- Burn lavender as incense to promote sleep, a meditative state, or to enhance your psychic powers (page 167).

- Scatter lavender blossoms around your home or incorporate it into a room spray to promote a sense of calm, well-being, and peace.

- Add blossoms or lavender tincture (page 127, variation) to a purification ritual bath (page 173).

- Wear a perfume that contains real lavender to attract love, deepen a friendship, encourage reconciliation, or repel negative energies.

- Inhale the scent of lavender frequently, to promote happiness and longevity.

- Lavender is associated with wish divination. Sprinkle some blossoms around the base of birthday cake candles to make the wish of the birthday person come true.

- Make lavender cookies or scones and eat them to promote happiness.

- Place lavender blossoms around the base of your crystal ball to encourage heightened psychic visions.

Lavender Projects

Rose Petal Simple Syrup (variation, page 115)

Vanilla Rose Moon Milk (variation, page 122)

Peppermint-Infused Medicinal Honey (variation, page 123)

Dandelion Tincture (variation, page 127)

Lavender Glycerite (page 130)

Dandelion and Plantain All-Purpose Healing Salve (variation, page 138)

Woodland Whipped Body Butter (variation, page 143)

Rosemary and Lavender Dry Spray Shampoo (page 147)

Spell Jars (page 159)

Intentional Tea Blends (page 161)

Candle Dressing (page 163)

Herbal and Resin Incense (page 167)

Smoke-Cleansing Bouquet (page 170)

Wheel of the Year Ritual Baths (page 173)

Black Salt (page 175)

Flying Ointment (page 178)

Magickal Mist (page 181)

Wildcrafted Witch's Broom (page 183)

Mint (*Mentha* spp.)

FOLK NAMES: Garden Mint, Common Mint, Lamb Mint, Brandy Mint

FAMILY: Lamiaceae

ASTROLOGY: Mercury, Virgo

ELEMENT: Air

PLANT LORE: Ancient Egyptians, Romans, and Greeks cultivated peppermint and used its leaves to treat indigestion and to soothe upset stomachs. Mint was also used by Greeks in their funerary practices to mask the scent of death. Mint was formed into toothpaste as early as the fourteenth century in Europe and was most likely brought to the New World by the Pilgrims.

MAGICKAL CORRESPONDENCES: money, luck, prosperity and abundance, healing, happiness, anti-jealousy, travel, protection, purification, cleansing negative energies, sexual energy, clear thinking, psychic and verbal communication, creativity

Identification

Mint, in the *Mentha* genus, comes in hundreds of different flowering varieties. These square-stemmed herbs are easy to grow and prefer moist, well-drained soil, and full sun to partial sun. Grow them outdoors during the summertime or indoors in a bright, sunny window any time of year. Mint plants are highly invasive. Grow them in container gardens or isolated, spacious, more wild areas where you won't mind if they take off—and trust me, they will.

Spearmint is the variety that you typically find in the grocery store and what is generally called "mint." It has light green, arrow-shaped leaves, green stems, and that classic sweet, minty flavor.

Peppermint is similar in appearance, with darker green leaves and a purplish-brown stem. It contains more menthol than spearmint, which gives it that strong, zingy flavor. Other more unusual varieties add interest to culinary kitchen witchery. Look for chocolate, apple (also called *woolly mint*), pineapple, lemon, lavender, banana, orange, and even strawberry mint; these taste as their names imply.

PARTS USED: aerial parts (mainly leaves and flowers)

Medicinal and Culinary Uses

Mint can soothe an upset stomach, relieve gas, quiet a cough, provide relief for a sore throat, soothe sinus inflammation, and alleviate congestion associated with the common cold, flu, and seasonal allergies. Mint is packed with vitamin A and vitamin C and can help build a stronger immune system. Mint even curbs hiccups. A lavender and mint tea is good for calming the nerves. Menthol (which peppermint produces more of than spearmint), provides a cooling, mildly anesthetic sensation when applied to the mouth or skin. And the menthol action in peppermint reduces inflammation; it cools and warms, so there's immediate relief on contact while the medicinal properties penetrate and soothe the skin.

- Simply smelling fresh mint can alleviate nausea or have an energizing effect.

- Drink a cup of mint tea or suck on a strong pastille to soothe indigestion. Use fresh or dried: 1 heaping teaspoon of dried tea per 1 cup (235 ml) of boiling water, or 10 fresh mint leaves per cup. Allow it to steep 10 to 15 minutes. Mint tea also makes an excellent skin wash or hair rinse for the scalp.

- Craft a tincture or glycerite made of fresh mint (page 127, variation, and page 130, variation).

- Breathe in a vapor steam, make a medicinal honey (page 123) or syrup (page 115, variation), or create a chest rub in the form of a salve (page 138, variation).

- Mint's anti-itch properties are ideal for bug bites, rashes, skin irritations, dry skin, and itchy scalp. Create a mint salve or mint-and-plantain salve (page 138, variation).

- Use the recipe for the Yarrow Clear-Skin Topical Spray, substituting mint for yarrow (page 145).

- Use peppermint in a topical spray to repel mosquitoes.

- Prepare mint as a tea or topical application to alleviate joint and muscle pain, ease headaches, relax muscles, or reduce menstrual cramps: Rub a few leaves on the forehead and temples, or make a tea-soaked cloth compress. Try herb-infused body and massage oils (page 131), body butter (page 143, variation), topical spray (page 145, variation), salve (page 138, variation), or balm (page 141).

- Refresh tired feet with a peppermint foot soak in the form of warm or cooled tea or a salve (page 138, variation).

- Mint tea has the antiseptic and disinfecting properties to be used as a clean-smelling floor wash.

- Chew on a fresh sprig of mint from the garden to kill the bacteria that cause bad breath.

- Craft flavored lip balms with chocolate, orange, or pineapple mint (page 141). They make great gifts!

- Infuse fresh chocolate mint in whipping cream for a few hours, strain out the leaves, and then whip it up for a delightful dessert topping. Minty desserts help prevent indigestion after a big meal.

- Peppermint-infused honey (page 123) tastes like candy and compliments many herbal teas— or you can eat it by the spoonful like I do.

- A sauce made with chopped spearmint and vinegar enhances lamb and poultry. I like to combine 1 cup (30 g) fresh spearmint leaves (finely chopped), 1 tablespoon (15 g) brown sugar, 3 tablespoons (45 ml) white wine vinegar, 4 tablespoons (60 ml) boiling water, and a pinch of salt.

- Add extra dimension and flavor to your sweet and savory dishes with mint. Use mint to cool the effects of spicy foods.

- Spearmint makes a tasty garnish in mojitos, mint juleps, or mint iced tea.

- Apple mint makes a yummy jelly or jam.

Magickal Uses

Mint can attract wealth and encourage smart money management. It can also invite high-vibrational deities, guides, or spirits that can aid you in your magickal practice. Use mint to cleanse negative energy and bless your space. Mint can enhance spirit communication and unleash sexual energy.

- Place a few mint leaves in the wealth corner of your home. According to feng shui, the money corner is in the southeast corner of your home or workspace.

- Make a bouquet of sprigs of fresh mint, lavender, and rosemary; mint is especially pretty when it is flowering. Place it on your altar or in your sacred space.

- Hang bundles of mint around your home to cleanse it and invite positive energies. The stronger the mint, the better. Peppermint is ideal because of its higher menthol content.

- Cleanse your magickal tools and crystals by rubbing them with a sprig of fresh mint.

- Sip mint tea or burn dried mint as an incense to promote clear thinking when setting intentions for spellwork (page 167).

- Place a mint leaf under your pillow to encourage psychic dreams.

- Add a few mint leaves to your luggage to ensure it gets to the correct destination. Keep a sprig in your car for safe travels.

- Spritz bed sheets with a mint linen spray to unleash passion. Use the Yarrow Clear-Skin Topical Spray recipe to create it (page 145).

- Dress candles with a few drops of heat-safe oil (any oils used for high-temp cooking) and crushed mint. Burn them for spells that involve any of the above magickal correspondences (page 163).

Mint Projects

Rose Petal Simple Syrup (variation, page 115)

Vanilla Rose Moon Milk (variation, page 122)

Peppermint-Infused Medicinal Honey (page 123)

Dandelion Tincture (variation, page 127)

Lavender Glycerite (variation, page 130)

Dandelion and Plantain All-Purpose Healing Salve (variation, page 138)

Vanilla Chocolate Mint Lip Balm (page 141)

Woodland Whipped Body Butter (variation, page 143)

Spell Jars (page 159)

Intentional Tea Blends (page 161)

Candle Dressing (page 163)

Herbal and Resin Incense (page 167)

Smoke-Cleansing Bouquet (page 170)

Wheel of the Year Ritual Baths (page 173)

Black Salt (page 175)

Flying Ointment (page 178)

Wildcrafted Witch's Broom (page 183)

Basil (*Ocimum basilicum*)

FOLK NAMES: Witches Herb, Common Basil, French Basil, Royal Herb, St. Josephwort

FAMILY: Lamiaceae

ASTROLOGY: Mars, Aries, Scorpio

ELEMENT: Fire

PLANT LORE: Basil's name originates from the Greek word *basilikon*, which means king, as its aroma was said to be "fit for a king." In India, basil is used as a sacred funerary herb. Italians have strongly linked it to romantic love, and it is a European tradition to place bouquets of basil in the hands of the dead, to ensure a safe journey to the Spirit World.

MAGICKAL CORRESPONDENCES: astral projection, romantic love, money and good fortune, cleansing negative energies, protection, beginnings, beauty, happiness, harmony and keeping the peace

Identification

Basil is likely native to India and is cultivated worldwide. It is sensitive to cold, so performs as an annual in cooler climates. It's best known for its culinary uses and potent smell and flavor—often described as a cross between cloves and licorice. Basil's leaves are vibrantly green and ovate in shape (although some varieties are purple). It grows a thick taproot, and has small, delicate white flowers. Of the more than forty types of basil, sweet basil (Genovese basil) is the most common. Other varieties include cinnamon, purple, Thai, Christmas, lettuce leaf, lemon, and lime basils. Holy basil—a similar species, also known as *tulsi*—is prized for its powerful adaptogen properties that help the body respond to stress and disease.

PARTS USED: aerial parts (generally the leaves)

Medicinal and Culinary Uses

Inflammation in the body is at the root of many diseases, and basil's anti-inflammatory properties will reduce inflammation in the body. Basil is packed with antioxidants that support the immune system and can slow the effects of aging when consumed or applied topically. Studies show that it can naturally prevent cancer. Basil is antibacterial, antiviral, antifungal, and antimicrobial, which means that it fights bacteria, viruses, yeast, and mold. Use this kitchen herb in salads, sauces, with meats, pasta, and more. It makes a wonderful health tonic.

- Make a basil salve to alleviate joint pain, heal wounds, prevent infection, and ease menstrual cramps (page 138, variation).

- Make a basil cough-and-cold syrup (page 115, variation) or infused honey (page 123) to quiet coughs and clear mucus. You can also gargle a concoction made of strong basil tea and salt.

- Create an all-purpose cleaner. Use the Magickal Mist recipe, substituting basil or combining it with the lavender, sage, and rosemary called for in the recipe (page 181).

- Promote clear skin with an antioxidant and antibacterial basil face mask made of finely chopped basil leaves and a spoonful of plain yogurt. Basil increases circulation, so you'll be left with a rosy glow.

- Food as medicine: I make and freeze batches of basil and wild greens pesto (page 113) every fall for my family and me to enjoy all winter long

Magickal Uses

Basil will boost clairvoyance and promote astral projection and hedge riding (page 179). It will also help you to embrace change and new beginnings. Use it to draw in love, peace, and harmony.

- Display flowering basil arrangements at family gatherings to keep the peace.

- Basil makes a special offering for deities, to show thanks and to appease them.

- Rub basil on your skin to attract romantic love.

- Draw good fortune to your business. Place a sprig of basil above the shop door. If you have an online shop, place some in the space in which you work.

- Keep a pot of basil next to your front door to ward off negative energies.

- Burn dried basil and rose petals together as incense (page 167) to attract love, good fortune, and protection, which are magickal correspondences they have in common.

- Sip basil tea before otherworldly travel and spirit communication. Use 1 heaping teaspoon of dried herb or 10 fresh basil leaves per 1 cup (235 ml) of boiling water and allow to steep for 10 to 15 minutes.

- Attach a bundle of basil to your showerhead for a shower that restores your energy, enhances your beauty, and fills you with feelings of contentment.

Basil Projects

Rosemary (*Rosmarinus officinalis*)

FOLK NAMES: Compass Weed, Dew of the Sea, Garden Rosemary, Incensier (as it was often burned as incense), Mary's Mantle

FAMILY: Lamiaceae

ASTROLOGY: Sun, Leo

ELEMENT: Fire

PLANT LORE: *Ros* means dew and *marinus* means sea. The rosemary bush is native to the seacoast of the Mediterranean and North Africa and has been described as growing "where one can hear the sea." An old saying goes, "Where rosemary grows, the woman rules." Students in ancient Greece wore garlands of rosemary to improve their memory during exams. Couples wore them during their wedding ceremonies to help recall their vows. In the fourteenth century, it was common practice to wash the feet of a robber with rosemary root to cure the person of their thievery ways. Rosemary is known for remembrance and used as such in the burial ritual of Shakespeare's Juliet. French hospitals burned rosemary and juniper to clean stagnant air. English botanist, herbalist, and doctor Nicholas Culpepper (1616–1654), referred to this herb as a cure-all remedy.

MAGICKAL CORRESPONDENCES: love, friendship, remembrance, ancestors, feminine power, driving out unwanted energies, purification, protection, faithfulness, memory, anti-gossip, intellect, invigoration, youth

Identification

Rosemary grows as a small evergreen shrub and has fine needles for leaves. This woody cultivated plant is available throughout the world and is widely used for cooking, especially for flavoring savory dishes. It has an earthy, woodsy, pungent fragrance that some liken to a blend of pine and lemon. Once you've handled fresh rosemary, its heavenly smell will stay on your hands. It produces tiny flower clusters of purple, pink, or white, and it prefers full sun and sandy, well-drained soil. For those who live in colder climates, you can grow this shrub in a container that you keep outdoors in summer and indoors in a bright, sunny window during winter.

PARTS USED: leaves

Medicinal and Culinary Uses

This herb is both warming and soothing, relaxing and invigorating. Just like other plants in the Lamiaceae family, rosemary has anti-inflammatory properties, and has even been reported to help with Restless Legs Syndrome. Studies also show that rosemary prevents neuronal cell death, which has promising implications for Alzheimer's disease. Culinary uses of rosemary help in the digestion of starchy foods.

- Drink rosemary tea or take a whiff of a sprig when studying or working on a project that requires serious brain power. For tea, use 1 heaping teaspoon of dried herb or double the amount for fresh herb per 1 cup (235 ml) of boiling water, steep 10 to 15 minutes.

- Blend rosemary with mint to make a pain salve or massage oil (page 138, variation) or an herb-infused oil (page 131). Either could be used as a chest rub to help break up congestion.

- Make a rosemary hair rinse (use tea) or an infused conditioning oil (page 131 for infused oil instructions). Rosemary has been known to stimulate hair growth, boosting circulation in the scalp. It has hair darkening properties, so you may wish to avoid it if you have light hair.

- Place a few rosemary sprigs in a hot bath to melt away tension and bodily aches and pains.

- Create a household cleaner and take advantage of rosemary's disinfectant properties. Add sprigs of rosemary to a blend of vinegar and water. Try the recipe for Magickal Mist, substituting rosemary, or adding it to the recipe's herbal blend (page 181).

- Rosemary makes a delicious seasoning, dried or fresh, that compliments chicken, potatoes, duck, lamb, seafood, soups, and even beverages, such as gin and tonic or lemonade.

Magickal Uses

Rosemary attracts helpful green energies to your garden. Plant rosemary in the garden to call garden fairies and elves; they protect the plants and help them grow. Rosemary also helps ward off gossip and is especially effective for promoting clarity.

- Use rosemary in anti-gossip spellwork. Keep a sprig in your place of work if employees are prone to cattiness. Put some in your pocket when going to a party.

- Burn smoke-cleansing bundles (page 170) of rosemary branches at Samhain, when the veil is thin, to promote clear communication with your ancestors. Use them to cleanse away negative energy before beginning your solo séance.

- Raise energy for spellwork, provide clarity for intention setting, or purify your ritual space by burning rosemary or sprinkling some in your ritual space. I cast a circle with a rosemary herbal bundle that I use as a wand (page 167 and page 170).

- Cleanse your magickal tools with rosemary after each use.

- Rosemary can be a substitute for frankincense, as they share similar properties. This made sense in ancient times, as frankincense was exotic, precious, and expensive.

Rosemary Projects

Rose Petal Simple Syrup (variation, page 115)

Pine Oxymel with Wild Apple Cider Vinegar (variation, page 117)

Peppermint-Infused Medicinal Honey (variation, page 123)

Dandelion Tincture (variation, page 127)

Lavender Glycerite (variation, page 130)

Dandelion and Plantain All-Purpose Healing Salve (variation, page 138)

Woodland Whipped Body Butter (variation, page 143)

Rosemary and Lavender Dry Spray Shampoo (page 147)

Intentional Tea Blends (page 161)

Candle Dressing (page 163)

Herbal and Resin Incense (page 167)

Smoke-Cleansing Bouquet (page 170)

Wheel of the Year Ritual Baths (page 173)

Black Salt (page 175)

Cauldron Simmering Potpourri (page 177)

Magickal Mist (page 181)

Wildcrafted Witch's Broom (page 183)

Sage (*Salvia officinalis*)

FOLK NAMES: Garden Sage, Golden Sage, Kitchen Sage, True Stage

FAMILY: Lamiaceae

ASTROLOGY: Jupiter, Sagittarius

ELEMENT: Air

PLANT LORE: Sage has a long, rich history of use for both medicinal and culinary purposes. In ancient times, it was used to banish evil, to increase fertility, and as a remedy for snakebites. Romans called it the "holy herb" and used it for healing skin, for cleaning teeth, and for supporting memory and increasing mental agility. They hung sage on the bedposts of newly married couples to bless their marriage and home life. The Greeks believed that eating sage gave you access to divine wisdom and promoted longevity, and even immortality. In the Middle Ages in France, Charlemagne recognized the benefits of this plant and cultivated it in his gardens.

MAGICKAL CORRESPONDENCES: longevity, protection, cleansing negative energy, wisdom, clarity, wishes, grief support, energy, happiness, business decisions

note

White sage (a different species) is being overharvested and is needed by Native Americans for specific sacred ceremonies. Garden sage is a perfectly good substitute.

Identification

As is common for the plants of the Lamiaceae family, sage is native to the Mediterranean region. It was cultivated by ancient Greeks, Romans, and Egyptians and naturalized worldwide. Sage is a small evergreen shrub with woody stems, grayish-green leaves covered in silvery down, with lavender-colored blooms (sometimes with white, pink, or purple flowers). There are more than 750 varieties. Modern cultivars come in other colors such as cream, yellow, purple, and rose. I enjoy using the beautiful tricolor variety, which I obtain from a local farmer. Sage prefers full sun and well-drained, loamy soil.

PARTS USED: aerial parts

Medicinal and Culinary Uses

Remember that food is medicine. In studies, this herb has been shown to balance cholesterol and help with menopausal hot flashes. Medical studies show it may be helpful for diabetics, as it boosts insulin action. Studies also support the use of sage to help dementia patients become more alert and calmer. Sage-infused honey has powerful medicinal properties; it's one of the best natural antibiotics. Sage's astringent properties can help with diarrhea and vomiting.

- Make a sage tea using 1 teaspoon dried herb or 10 fresh leaves per 1 cup (235 ml) of boiling water and allow to steep 10 to 15 minutes. Gargle with sage tea to ease a sore throat and treat laryngitis. Sage tea can also help with canker sores or bleeding gums.

- Use sage tea as a hair rinse or hair oil to prevent hair loss (page 131, instructions for infused oil). Combine it with rosemary, which increases circulation and hair growth. Both of these herbs will darken hair, so are best suited for dark hair or for people who wish to darken their gray hair.

- Use sage-infused honey (page 123, variation) to alleviate cough and cold symptoms.

- Use a topical application for cuts and scrapes, or even eczema. Topical possibilities are as a salve (page 138, variation), a tea wash, or a compress with herbs tightly bound in fabric, steamed, and applied to the affected area.

- To treat acne or oily skin, make a yogurt and sage face mask. Blend some finely chopped herb and combine with a spoonful of plain yogurt.

- Sage calms a nervous tummy. Sip sage tea before an interview, audition, or speech.

Magickal Uses

Burn sage to cleanse your space and provide protection, to encourage favorable business dealings and decisions, or uplift and energize you. Sage provides grief support. Sage is associated with wish divination.

- Burn a bundle of garden sage to help cleanse your space and clear your mind for spellwork (page 170).

- Keep a small jar of dry garden sage and give it a whiff if you're feeling blue.

- Create a wreath with sage, lavender, and rosebuds and hang it on your door for home protection.

- Create a spell jar containing sage and pink quartz for unconditional love and healing (page 159). Sage is an ideal plant for using in healing-based spellwork, as it is a plant of longevity.

- Write a wish on a slip of paper and burn it with dried sage, sending your wish out into the Universe.

Sage Projects

Pine Oxymel with Wild Apple Cider Vinegar (variation, page 117)

Peppermint-Infused Medicinal Honey (variation, page 123)

Dandelion Tincture (variation, page 127)

Dandelion and Plantain All-Purpose Healing Salve (variation, page 138)

Woodland Whipped Body Butter (variation, page 143)

Spell Jars (page 159)

Intentional Tea Blends (page 161)

Candle Dressing (page 163)

Herbal and Resin Incense (page 167)

Smoke-Cleansing Bouquet (page 170)

Wheel of the Year Ritual Baths (page 173)

Black Salt (page 175)

Magickal Mist (page 181)

Wildcrafted Witch's Broom (page 183)

CHAPTER 4

Meet the Plants
Wild Plants

Wild plants are what many think of as weeds, although green witches appreciate them for their wild wisdom, their healing and culinary properties, and their magick. Foraging, herbalism, and the art of cooking with wild edibles continues to grow in popularity, reaching more and more people. Dandelion greens, for instance, are now being offered in grocery stores. Foraged mushrooms are served in restaurants. Local adult education centers are offering classes in foraging and herbalism. For me, diving into wildcrafting and herbalism took nothing more than an inspiring bite of a tender broadleaf plantain leaf at my first foraging class. It was so full of bold flavor—nutty, rich, with a tinge of bitterness— unlike any vegetable I had ever tasted. I'll be forever smitten with the weeds, and I hope to give others a "taste," through my teaching, so they too will be forever hooked.

Dandelion (*Taraxacum officinale*)

FOLK NAMES: Witch Gowan, Lion's Tooth, Blowball, Piss-a-Bed, Wild Endive

FAMILY: Asteraceae

ASTROLOGY: Jupiter, Sagittarius

ELEMENT: Air

PLANT LORE: Fossilized dandelion seeds found in southern Russia date to the Pliocene period, about 30 million years ago. Ancient Greeks, Romans, and Egyptians used dandelions for food and medicine, and dandelions have been significant in Chinese medicine. The Yoruba of Africa use dandelion in their holistic approach to medicine, which has been in existence for more than 4,000 years. Not native to North America, dandelion was most likely brought over by the Pilgrims and used as food and medicine. Through colonization, the dandelion naturalized quickly. This plant now propagates as a wildflower. According to ancient lore, if a dandelion seed comes to you on the wind, it means that a good spirit is bringing you a message.

MAGICKAL CORRESPONDENCES: psychic powers, divination, spirit communication, wishes, luck, wealth, friendship, joy, beginnings, courage, resilience

Identification

Dandelion grows everywhere in the world except Antarctica. It's in lawns, fields, roadsides, and sidewalk cracks. It grows from a basal rosette, has a smooth and hollow light-green stem that eventually turns a purplish brown, has jagged-edged leaves, and a bright yellow flower head made up of numerous smaller flowers called florets. It blooms in spring and provides the first nectar of the season to pollinators, especially the honeybee and bumblebee. Then it blooms once again in later summer, in smaller amounts.

It is best to harvest roots after the first frost, as that is when the plant's medicine goes to the roots, before hibernation. Early spring is another ideal time to harvest the roots, before the plant forms aerial parts. You'll have better luck extracting dandelion roots from looser, less compacted soil. Using a garden trowel, dig down and around the roots with care, loosening them. Gently wiggle and pull your roots from the ground. You can dry roots in a dehydrator and reconstitute them for soups and stews all winter.

PARTS USED: whole plant, including the root

Medicinal and Culinary Uses

If I was ever stranded on a deserted island and only allowed one thing, I would choose dandelion! The entire plant (including the root and seeds) is edible and has everything you need to live and thrive. It's considered a complete protein, as it has eight essential amino acids and B vitamins. It's packed with vitamin A, C, E, K, calcium, potassium, iron, magnesium, copper, and zinc, due to its deep taproot that accesses so much goodness from the soil.

Dandelion balances electrolytes and helps with the absorption of other nutrients. Dandelion will encourage a healthy gut; reduce inflammation; aid in digestion of proteins and fats; purify, build, and oxygenate the blood; decongest the liver and improve its function (which improves skin and age spots); reduce acidity in the body; and increase the flow of urine to flush out toxins and lower blood pressure without depleting potassium.

- Toss dandelion in a salad. Blossoms taste sweet and mildly of honey, and young, tender leaves are less bitter. You can also add the leaves to Wild Greens Pesto (page 113), along with plantain and basil. Or toss them in a stir fry, steam them, or quickly boil them.

- Wildcraft a whole-plant tincture in the fall for use in the colder months (page 127).

- Dry dandelion leaves for tea. Or try a caffeine-free coffee substitute made of roasted dandelion root (page 121).

- Use the milky sap from the stem to heal pimples, warts, or sunspots.

- Use the blossoms to make wine, or you can pull them apart and place a handful of florets in your favorite muffin recipe.

- Make a highly moisturizing dandelion blossom facial serum (page 131).

- Try an all-purpose salve for healing skin and for pain relief (page 138).

Dumb Supper

Incorporate dandelion root into a dish served at a Dumb Supper, a tradition of Ireland and Great Britain used to beckon spirits on Samhain. Set a place at the table for the spirit or spirits who you wish to invite and hold the supper in silence so you may hear the whisperings of the spirits. I'll either reconstitute some dried dandelion root for a squash soup or make a dandelion root "coffee" for dessert with cloves, ginger, cinnamon, cardamom, vanilla, and almond milk (page 121).

Magickal Uses

Dandelion boosts psychic powers and has been known to invoke Hecate, the Greek goddess of witchcraft and ghosts.

- Drink dandelion root tea (often called "coffee") to enhance your divination practice, encourage prophetic dreaming, or to call spirits to you for spirit communication (page 121).

- Burn dried dandelion leaves as an incense to boost clairvoyance (page 167).

Dandelion Projects

Wild Greens Pesto (page 113)

Pine Oxymel with Wild Apple Cider Vinegar (variation, page 117)

Roasted Dandelion Root Coffee (page 121)

Dandelion Tincture (page 127)

Lavender Glycerite (variation, page 130)

Dandelion and Plantain All-Purpose Healing Salve (page 138)

Vanilla Chocolate Mint Lip Balm (variation, page 141)

Woodland Whipped Body Butter (variation, page 143)

Spell Jars (page 159)

Intentional Tea Blends (page 161)

Candle Dressing (page 163)

Herbal and Resin Incense (page 167)

Smoke-Cleansing Bouquet (page 170)

Wheel of the Year Ritual Baths (page 173)

Wildcrafted Witch's Broom (page 183)

Broadleaf Plantain (*Plantago major*)

FOLK NAMES: Cuckoo's Bread, The Leaf of Patrick, Englishman's Foot, Ripple Grass, Waybread

FAMILY: Plantaginaceae

ASTROLOGY: Venus, Taurus

ELEMENT: Earth

PLANT LORE: Plantain (the broadleaf plantain, not the variety of banana) is a wild edible that grows underfoot worldwide, appearing in pastures and along pathways. In the tenth century, Anglo-Saxons included plantain as a sacred plant in their *Nine Herbs Charm*, and Native American tribes of North America have called it "life medicine." An example of its early use is seen in Shakespeare's *Romeo and Juliet*, where there is a reference to plantain being used to treat a broken leg bone. Along the lines of magickal lore, carrying a plantain root in one's pocket would prevent a snake bite.

MAGICKAL CORRESPONDENCES: protection, healing, strength, invisibility, vitality, freedom

Identification

There are thirty-four species of plantain found worldwide, all edible and medicinal, available spring through fall. Its leaves are shaped like the bottom of a foot, and its name is derived from the Latin *planta*, meaning sole of the foot. Interestingly, it grows where people and animals tread—on pathways, pastures, lawns, and unpaved driveways. The plant is made up of a group of richly green, deep-veined, egg-shaped leaves (similar to spinach leaves) that grow from a rosette. Inside the stems you'll find a stringy fiber, which helps in making a positive identification. Plantain has a robust flavor that's mildly nutty and slightly bitter. The smaller, younger ones taste less bitter and have a less chewy texture. The flowering stalks contain seeds that make a tasty trail snack.

PARTS USED: whole plant, including the root and seeds

Medicinal and Culinary Uses

When my family and I go camping, I search for a patch of plantain at our site, as it's a powerful natural first aid for many needs. In emergency situations, plantain may be used to purify water. I craft a plantain tincture and dry some for tea to have on hand in my herbal apothecary for cold and flu season as an expectorant. Plantain makes a highly nutritious food with many health benefits: It has iron, zinc, copper, calcium, fiber, protein, potassium, omega-3 fatty acids, and vitamins A, C, and K. It increases bone density and strengthens teeth, promotes healthy elimination, protects the body from free radical damage, strengthens the immune system, and lowers cholesterol.

- Make an instant poultice by chewing some leaves into a paste and placing it on the skin to draw out toxins from bug bites or to treat poison ivy, stop the bleeding of cuts, disinfect an injury and prevent infection, reduce inflammation, and promote healing.

- Craft an all-purpose salve or balm (page 138) for first aid or for soothing sunburn, healing chapped skin, and relieving pain.

- Use plantain in a lip balm (page 141, variation).

- Make a healing foot soak after a hike by combining a handful of fresh, chopped plantain leaves and warm water in a foot basin.

- To clear mucus from the respiratory tract, mix a little honey with a plantain tincture to make cough syrup (page 127) or make a simple syrup with plantain (page 115, variation).

- Use plantain as a mouthwash to kill bacteria that causes bad breath and to tighten gums. Follow the recipe for the Yarrow Clear-Skin Topical Spray to make the mouthwash, substituting plantain for yarrow (page 145).

- Add plantain leaves to a wild greens pesto (page 113) with dandelion leaves and basil.

- Create a plantain "juice" by blending a handful of leaves with 2 cups (470 ml) of cold water, straining out the plant matter, and sweetening the drink with raw honey or apple juice.

- Try a plantain infusion: Brew 1 ounce (28 g) of dried herb per 1 quart (1 L) of water for 4 hours.

- Make plantain chips (like kale chips) by coating the leaves with olive oil, sprinkling on a bit of salt, and baking on a cookie sheet at 350°F (175°C, or gas mark 4) for about 10 minutes, until they are crispy.

- Blend the leaves into your favorite smoothie.

- Grind dried plantain leaf into a powder that you add to smoothies or sauces.

- Toss tender plantain leaves into a mixed greens salad with apples, raisins, and walnuts.

- Add tender plantain leaves to spring rolls.

- Dry the plantain roots and reconstitute them all winter in soups and stews.

Magickal Uses

Plantain has invisibility power. Historically, it has been used to protect one's home from thieves. Use plantain with your spellwork to amplify its power.

- Place a plantain leaf in your shoe before walking a long distance or exercising, to keep you strong and energetic.

- Keep a small bag of dried plantain in your car to serve as a protective charm.

- Place a bundle in each corner of your home.

- Carry some plantain with you if you're going somewhere where you wish to be unnoticed and left alone.

- Wrap your wand in fresh plantain leaves, secured with a piece of twine.

Broadleaf Plantain Projects

Wild Greens Pesto (page 113)

Peppermint-Infused Medicinal Honey (variation, page 123)

Dandelion Tincture (variation, page 127)

Lavender Glycerite (variation, page 130)

Dandelion and Plantain All-Purpose Healing Salve (page 138)

Vanilla Chocolate Mint Lip Balm (variation, page 141)

Woodland Whipped Body Butter (variation, page 143)

Spell Jars (page 159)

Wheel of the Year Ritual Baths (page 173)

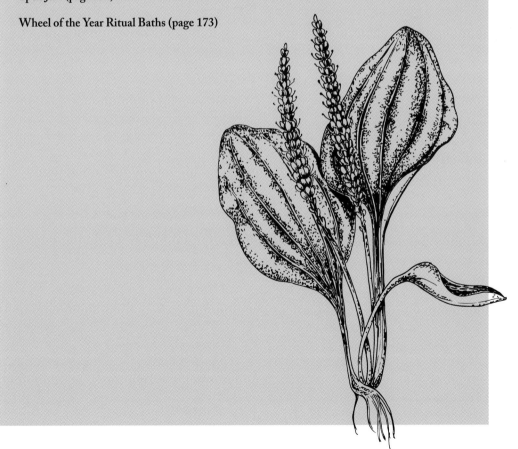

Mugwort (*Artemisia vulgaris*)

FOLK NAMES: Artemis Herb, Cronewort, Moxa, Sailor's Tobacco

FAMILY: Asteraceae

ASTROLOGY: Moon, Venus, Capricorn

ELEMENT: Earth

PLANT LORE: Roman soldiers put mugwort in their sandals to prevent fatigue. In the Middle Ages, mugwort was used to protect travelers from evil spirits and dangerous animals. The Anglo-Saxons included mugwort in their tenth-century *Nine Herbs Charm*. Mugwort has long been used in Chinese medicine to increase the flow of qi throughout the body using a process called moxibustion, where the plant is burned on top of acupuncture needles. Mugwort most likely came to North America on sixteenth-century ships. Fun fact: Each mugwort plant contains approximately 200,000 seeds.

MAGICKAL CORRESPONDENCES: psychic powers, astral projection and hedge riding, vivid dreams and visions, cleansing negative energy, protection, strength, healing, fertility, safe travels

Identification

Mugwort is native to Europe and Asia and naturalized all around the world. It's often confused with the plant wormwood; they are related, but not the same plant. Mugwort grows to be 3 to 6 feet (1 to 2 meters) tall, has purple-tinged stems, and has leaves that get smaller as they go up the stem. The leaves smell like mint and cinnamon, are lobed with pointed tips, and are green on top and white with fine hairs on the bottom. The flower heads, called *panicles*, form in reddish-brown, round clusters, from mid to late summer. Mugwort thrives in moist to somewhat dry soil, requires full to partial sun, and grows happily on the edges of forests, roadsides, disturbed land, and even sidewalk cracks. The leaves can be eaten raw or cooked, and are best harvested in mid-spring, before they become too bitter. For medicinal purposes, harvest in the summer, for increased potency.

PARTS USED: whole plant, including the root

Medicinal and Culinary Uses

As a nervine, mugwort relaxes the body and can be used to promote restful sleep, for meditation, and in other spiritual work. Mugwort acts as an expectorant, and the plant repels insects such as mosquitoes and moths. Mugwort is used for seasoning meat, fish, noodles, and drinks. Historically, it was used to flavor beer, before the discovery of hops, and has made a comeback with the popularity of unique artisan beers. Traditionally it's used in poultry stuffing. Mugwort stimulates the appetite, aids in digestion, and acts as a diuretic, flushing impurities out of the body. Tea is made from the plant's leaves, flowers, and roots.

- Combine mugwort tincture with honey to make a cough syrup or use the recipe for the Rose Petal Simple Syrup on page 115, substituting mugwort for rose petals.

- Burn mugwort as incense to ward off mosquitoes (page 167). Put the leaves anywhere you would place mothballs or cedar blocks.

- Make a salve of mugwort to repel bugs, keep minor wounds from getting infected, ease pain, and help heal bruises faster (page 138, variation).

after the...
many...
relation...
various...
general...
not...
the animal bodie...
like subjects I shall...
what I want to...
charts before I...
point from a somewhat...
the facts may finally... the pub...
useful in satisfying us what is prof...
mentals of our business...

Now that involved a great deal of work.
take down from my shel...
report issued by the fifty cen... experiment or...
every experiment m... with young steers or sh...
whether in my judg... accurate...
planned, and the facts... time to take...
experiment; and I took th... young...
hired by the hour to ma... worked out...
tain number of figures.

The remainder of what I have to say...
cipally the explanation of these charts, and a...
based upon them as you may wish to...
these headings, cows for the production of milk, swine fo... rowth,
bovine for growth, (mostly steers at various ages,—but t... exper-
ment in fattening cows) and sheep for growth. It is interesting to
note the number of states in which these reliable experiments have
been carried on. In twenty states experiment stations have carried
on experiments with regard to the production of milk; in thirteen
states with regard to the growth of steers; and in five states with
regard to the growth of lambs. The experiments which I used
...ded 60 with cows, 277 with swine, 31 with steers and 12 with
...p; making 380 different experiments that had to be reviewed,
...ing 2140 animals. Now, friends, I think you will agree with
...t so far as averages mean anything,—and a great deal of
call the fundamental exact data of the world comes from
—there is a pretty good mass of material; 380 experi-
...lving results with 2140 animals. Now what did I have

...t my data? I had to get in each experiment
...and the kind of food; and in most cases the
...had to use the amount of food and its
... of the animal, or the milk produced and
...milk
...experiment and calculate the amount
...pared blanks and sent to every exper-
... you experiments had been made, and said,
...er to us... you please calculate these results as I ask
...with the help of one or two young men. We cal-
...experiment the amount of digestible food.
...digestible food, because it is of no use to take
...food as a basis of calculation or comparison.
...much does it take... port... pig as compared
...pig rate concentra...
...carboh... is not...
...digestible... ghly digestible,
...amda... You have got
...takes care of
...ount of digesti-
...als per 1,000
...med in one day
...estible food, and the
...at you are feeding
...ght... an you are
... have fed to
...spond... 18 pounds of
...th... pounds of digesti-
...the... stands
... a pretty

...what is the relation...
pr... that is going to...
pr... 100 pounds of...
... namely 13 per... milk.
...p. For 10 pound...
food; for 10 po...
live weight of...

In oth...

Magickal Uses

Mugwort is revered by many witches and is sacred to the Greek goddess Artemis. Use this magickal herb to encourage and enhance psychic ability for divination practices, spirit communication, and astral projection. Mugwort is a bitter, so you'll want to sweeten your tea with honey or with maple syrup (my favorite). Maple is associated with "flying," so will enhance the power of the tea. I make a "flying ointment" that contains mugwort, which I apply to pulse points and the Third Eye half an hour before spiritual practice (page 178).

- Thirty minutes before your practice, sip mugwort tea (steep 1 teaspoon of dried leaves and flowers or double the amount for fresh, in 1 cup (235 ml) of boiling water for 10 to 15 minutes) or take a teaspoon of mugwort tincture (page 127, variation). You can also take a mugwort herbal ritual bath to serve the same purpose, by adding a handful of leaves and blossoms to the bathwater.

- Place a mugwort dream pillow near your bed or put leaves in your pillowcase to encourage vivid dreams. Keep a mugwort dream journal at your bedside, for jotting down those mugwort-induced, colorful dreams.

- Cleanse and charge your divination tools—crystal ball, tarot cards, runes, pendulum, scrying bowl—with mugwort. Rub leaves on them or pass them through its smoke (page 167 or page 170).

- Dress candles (page 163) with anointing oil and crushed, dried mugwort. Burn them during your divination practice or spirit communication session.

- Craft a spell jar (page 159) filled with mugwort and amethyst and place it next to your bed to encourage psychic dreams. You can place it in your car for safe travels, or next to you during an astral projection session, or use it to make a protective amulet for a loved one setting out on a journey.

Mugwort Projects

Peppermint-Infused Medicinal Honey (variation, page 123)

Dandelion Tincture (variation, page 127)

Lavender Glycerite (variation, page 130)

Dandelion and Plantain All-Purpose Healing Salve (variation, page 138)

Spell Jars (page 159)

Intentional Tea Blends (page 161)

Candle Dressing (page 163)

Herbal and Resin Incense (page 167)

Smoke-Cleansing Bouquet (page 170)

Wheel of the Year Ritual Baths (page 173)

Black Salt (page 175)

Cauldron Simmering Potpourri (page 177)

Flying Ointment (page 178)

Wildcrafted Witch's Broom (page 183)

Clover (*Trifolium* spp.)

FOLK NAMES: Honey, Three-Leaved Grass, Shamrock, Trefoil

FAMILY: Fabaceae

ASTROLOGY: Mercury, Taurus

ELEMENT: Air

PLANT LORE: Clover is considered a traditional magickal herb and is well known for its four-leafed clover connection to good luck. The three-leafed clover is associated with the witch's trinity of "maiden, mother, crone." Ancient Romans associated dreams of clover with happiness and good fortune. In the fifteenth through seventeenth centuries, peasants and knights wore clovers for protection. Three-leafed red and white clovers have been used extensively for medicinal and magickal purposes for centuries. Historically, red clover has been used in love and lust potions, to help with money and business dealings, and to banish negative spirits. White clover was worn to protect from hexes. Both three-leafed varieties were used to feed livestock and were used as a flour substitute.

MAGICKAL CORRESPONDENCES: love, lust, money, luck, abundance and prosperity, success, protection, cleansing negative energy, clarity, female energy, beauty, healing, fairies, clairvoyance

Identification

White clover is tinged with light pink. Red clover is not really red but either dark pink or pinkish-purple. Both form flower heads that look like pom-poms and are composed of individual florets. The stems and leaves are mildly fuzzy. Clover grows in a sprawling fashion across farmed fields, meadows, and lawns. It appears in early summer in large numbers and then consistently flowers throughout the summer in smaller amounts. Fun fact: Clover makes a wonderful source of nitrogen for soil.

PARTS USED: flowering heads and upper leaves

Medicinal and Culinary Uses

Red clover has many medicinal uses, from purifying blood to decongesting the lymphatic system and strengthening bones and teeth. It supports the respiratory system, is a natural estrogen that relieves menopausal symptoms such as hot flashes, eases joint pain, and tones the uterus. Current studies show that clover may prevent breast cancer. Red clover tea and stronger infusions may be consumed for medicinal reasons. Use completely fresh (not browned) blossoms to make a mildly sweet tea, which can be further sweetened with honey, to calm you while stimulating cognitive function. Fresh red and white blooms and upper leaves are wonderful in salads.

- Create a red clover salve (page 138, variation) to address joint pain and skin issues such as eczema, psoriasis, athlete's foot, bug bites, stings, and mild burns. It can be used as a breast massage salve, for lymphatic drainage.

- Make a clover face wash for acne: Steep either 1 heaping teaspoon of dried clover florets or 2 teaspoons (8.5 g) of fresh clover florets in 1 cup (235 ml) of boiling water for 10 to 15 minutes. Florets are the individual small flowers that make up the composite blossom head. Strain out plant matter and allow the tea to cool before use.

- Wildcraft a white and red clover blossom sun tea with mint and lemon. I add 1 cup (236 g) of fresh blossoms, 1 cup (236 g) of fresh mint, and slices from 1 lemon to a quart (1 L) of water and put it out in the sun for 3 to 4 hours.

- Pull the florets apart and sprinkle them over the salad or toss them in a grain bowl.

- Florets can also be dried and ground up in a coffee grinder to be used as a flour replacement. Use it in the Clover Blossom Banana Bread (page 121). The clover adds protein, a pleasing texture, and a mild sweetness to bread and muffins.

- Sprinkle the florets of clover blossoms in your vegetable garden add nitrogen to the soil.

Magickal Uses

Clover corresponds to powerful female energy. Use it to rid your space of negative energy, replacing it with vibrations of abundance, prosperity, and love. Red clover is often associated with healing rituals for sick or injured domesticated animals. Clover is also a potent grounding herb: Use it in the initial stages of spellwork to ground yourself firmly before raising energy for the spell.

- Brew and enjoy a tea with your lover made of red and white clover blossoms, peppermint, rose, and lavender—an herbal blend associated with love and lust. Use 1 teaspoon of fully dried clover blossoms or 2 tablespoons (5.5 g) of fresh ones per 1 cup (235 ml) of boiling water and steep 10 to 15 minutes.

- Add 1 cup (235 ml) of clover tea to your floor wash to promote a happy home.

- Infuse a few blossoms in a glass of water beneath the light of the moon, to create an elixir of beauty and feminine power. Drink the water in the morning to boost your radiant female self.

Clover Projects

Pine Oxymel with Wild Apple Cider Vinegar (variation, page 117)

Clover Blossom Banana Bread (page 120)

Peppermint-Infused Medicinal Honey (variation, page 123)

Dandelion Tincture (variation, page 127)

Dandelion and Plantain All-Purpose Healing Salve (variation, page 138)

Woodland Whipped Body Butter (variation, page 143)

Spell Jars (page 159)

Intentional Tea Blends (page 161)

Wheel of the Year Ritual Baths (page 173)

Wildcrafted Witch's Broom (page 183)

CHAPTER 5

Meet the Plants

Plants That Can Be Both Wild and Cultivated

Some plants are considered both wild and cultivated. Take the rose, for instance, of which many species can be found growing in the wild, surviving and thriving without human intervention, as well as hundreds of different varieties of hybrid roses used largely for ornamental purposes and cared for by human hand. The same goes for the apple tree, which comes in nearly 7,500 varieties—both wild and cultivated—and has been revered since ancient times by the Greeks, Romans, Hebrews, and Scandinavians as a provider of "golden" fruit and as a symbol of wisdom and peace. This chapter explores plants that grow both in the wild and as cultivars available in your local nurseries and greenhouses, including roses, yarrow, pine, and apple.

Rose (*Rosa* spp.)

FOLK NAMES: "A rose is a rose is a rose."
—Gertrude Stein

There are no other common names.

FAMILY: Rosaceae

ASTROLOGY: Venus, Moon

ELEMENT: Water

PLANT LORE: The rose has been revered through art, literature, and spiritual practices. Historically, the rose is a symbol of secrecy and trust and was hung from the ceiling over clandestine meetings to ensure no one would break the trust. Early Greeks and Romans viewed the rose as a symbol of love, passion, beauty, and purity. The Greek lyric poet Anacreon (570–488 BC) wrote that the seafoam from which Aphrodite was born transformed into a spray of white roses. When she attempted to help her injured lover Adonis, a few drops of her blood fell upon the white roses, turning them to a passionate and fiery red, as a symbol of their romantic love.

MAGICKAL CORRESPONDENCES: love, trust, passion, divination, healing, psychic powers, blessings, peace, happiness, protection, mending a broken heart

Identification

There are approximately 150 species of roses that grow either as herbaceous plants, climbers, shrubs, "trees," or groundcover. Technically, roses do not have thorns but rather, prickles, which grow on the outer layers of the stems. Actual thorns are rooted in the body of a stem. Wild roses are generally pink or white and have five petals that form one layer around a base that contains spiral stamens. Cultivated roses have multiple layers of petals. Roses bloom in early summer, and the wild ones can be found in sunny spots of wooded areas.

Foragers and herbalists enjoy the hardy, fragrant Rosa rugosa, which grows along the coastline. In the fall, roses produce rose hip fruits that grow from the base of the former bloom. When harvesting, leave some flowers behind for the pollinators and so they may become rose hips. Harvest rose hips after a frost for the most available medicine. Leave some rose hips behind for birds to eat and to reseed them naturally. Never use roses from florists. For pleasing and effective results, use only aromatic varieties.

PARTS USED: generally petals and rose hip fruit

WARNING: If using cultivated roses for medicinal and culinary purposes, make sure they have not been sprayed with pesticides. If you purchase them from a nursery, wait a year or two before using them.

Medicinal and Culinary Uses

Roses are analgesic and anti-inflammatory, which means that they can reduce inflammation and provide pain relief for sore muscles and joints and for pinched nerves. Rose is good for healing skin issues such as sunburns, minor burns, rashes, and minor cuts and scrapes. It has clotting properties that stop bleeding. Its aromatic properties calm and soothe, while its constituents help to heal. Rose petals and rose hips are high in bioflavonoids. Rose hips are packed with vitamins, A, C, E, B-complex, calcium, potassium, and magnesium. Dried rose petal tea is high in tannins, so similar to black tea in taste, but without the caffeine. Rose is cooling to the body and good

for the heart, both for the physical heart and the spirit. It has anxiety-reducing properties and can lift your mood.

- Make a rose petal–infused honey (page 123) with fresh-wilted petals for treating coughs and colds. If you add this honey to a liquor that is at least 35 proof, you'll have yourself an elixir (page 124). You can also make a rose tincture (page 127, variation) or glycerite (page 130, variation).

- Roses make wonderful ingredients for salves (page 138, variation), balms (page 141, variation), massage oils (page 131, infused oil instructions), body butters (page 143, variation), perfumes, and room and linen sprays.

- Use rose petals in a witch hazel toner. Roses are naturally astringent. Simply add a handful of dried petals to the toner, steep for 2 weeks, and strain out the plant matter.

- Create a rose petal–infused, skin-friendly oil to serve as a facial serum (page 131, infused oil instructions). It will soften and smooth skin and even out skin tone, reducing the look of sunspots.

- Sprinkle fresh rose petals on salads or make rose petal jelly, jam, wine, or syrup (page 115) for cocktails, mocktails, and for over ice cream.

Magickal Uses

Rose petals are associated with Aphrodite, goddess of love, and make a potent natural aphrodisiac. Rose petals have been used for love spells and potions for centuries. A bit on love spell ethics: Love spells can be used to enhance existing love or to call your lover to you but should never be used to manipulate or coerce another person. For more on love spells, see page 157.

- Create a rose petal–infused rosé wine for yourself as an act of self-love or to share with your lover. Simply combine a handful of fresh rose petals with the wine in a quart-sized (1-L) mason jar. Steep for about five days before straining and enjoying. I like to dip the rim of my wine glass in honey and coat it with chocolate shavings.

- Draw a luxurious rose petal ritual bath for yourself; fresh is best but dried will work too (page 173). Light some candles, play soft music, and sip a rose petal–infused wine. Bathe yourself in love, healing, protection, and peace.

- Try this ancient rose petal divination practice: Take three green rose leaves, each representing a potential lover/mate. The one that stays green the longest is "the one."

- Carry a small drawstring purse filled with rose petals for protection and to invite good luck wherever you go.

Rose Projects

Yarrow (*Achillea millefolium*)

FOLK NAMES: Millfoil, Soldier's Woundwort, Thousand Seal, Nosebleed, Devil's Nettle

FAMILY: Asteraceae

ASTROLOGY: Venus, Taurus

ELEMENT: Water

PLANT LORE: Yarrow is associated with Achilles, a gifted warrior in Greek mythology who was taught how to heal soldier's wounds with the plant. As recently as World War I, soldiers would carry yarrow for treating battle wounds, as it stopped bleeding, prevented infection, and healed tissue. Yarrow has been considered a lucky herb by the Chinese, and one that promotes intelligence. It was said to grow around the grave of Confucius. According to Scottish lore, rubbing one's eyelids with yarrow leaf granted second sight. Yarrow is also used in bouquets at weddings and handfastings. Several Native American nations used the plant as a remedy for toothaches, earaches, colds, pain, fever, and as a sleep aid. Historically, yarrow has been used in love divination spells to predict a future love or to test the potency of a current love.

MAGICKAL CORRESPONDENCES: love, psychic powers, prophetic and vivid dreams, strength, courage, cleansing negative energy, communication, healthy boundaries

Identification

Common yarrow (the true native species, white-flowered variety) is carbon dated at 60,000 years old and is native to Asia, Europe, and North America. You'll find this pollinator-pleasing plant growing in fields, pastures, lawns, roadsides, and even coastal places. Yarrow prefers sandy, loamy soil, and full sun. It is a robust drought- and heat-tolerant plant that spreads with ease. It has feathery, fern-like leaves that are evenly arranged in a spiral manner along a mildly hairy stem. The flower clusters (called *florescences*) are either grayish-white or pinkish-white. In this book, we will focus on common yarrow rather than the other colorful cultivated varieties developed for ornamental purposes. The cultivars have high volatile oils that are not safe for taking internally. I prefer to work with the original plant. Young leaves and flowers are edible.

PARTS USED: aerial parts

Medicinal and Culinary Uses

Yarrow stimulates appetite and aids in digestion. It reduces bacteria in the intestines and supports healthy blood circulation. Yarrow stops bleeding, prevents infection, promotes healing, and heals bruises and acne. It also has anti-inflammatory properties that are helpful for arthritis. Yarrow is a powerful antimicrobial and antiviral. Studies show it to be effective against five types of bacteria including staph, E. coli, and salmonella. The leaves have a strong, somewhat bitter taste; use them sparingly in salads and as an addition to a wild greens spring roll.

- Chew on a leaf to create an instant poultice that you can apply to a wound, or make a poultice with plant matter and a cloth.

- Incorporate yarrow into an all-purpose skin-healing salve (page 138, variation).

- Make a topical spray from 30 percent yarrow tincture and 70 percent distilled water (page 145). This spray can also be used as a bug repellent.

- Make a potent medicinal tea: 1 teaspoon dried yarrow leaf and blossoms per boiling cup (235 ml) of water, steep 10 to 15 minutes. The tea encourages sweating, which can help break a fever. It warms the blood and can kill viral and bacterial toxins.

- To stop nose bleeds simply roll a yarrow leaf up into a ball and place it in the nostril.

- Take a yarrow tincture to ease a heavy menstrual flow (page 127, variation).

Magickal Uses

Historically, hanging a yarrow bouquet over a bed as a wedding decoration ensured a lasting love of at least seven years. Yarrow encourages and amplifies psychic ability and attracts spirit ancestors with whom you wish to contact and connect. It draws in spirits that your Higher Self most wants to visit. Yarrow is worn for protection and courage. In the garden, yarrow protects other plants around it by warding off harmful insects.

- Make a wish upon the first yarrow blooms you see each summer.

- Brew a cup of yarrow tea and sip it before divination practice or a spirit communication session.

- Combine yarrow with mint, rose petals, and lavender, herbs which are also associated with psychic powers and communing with the Otherworld (page 161). Yarrow is bitter, so sweeten it with some honey.

- Make a dream pillow or spell jar (page 159) filled with yarrow and place it near your bed to encourage vivid, prophetic dreams.

- Keep a small bundle of yarrow at home, in your place of work, or on your person, to encourage healthy boundaries in relationships. It can also melt away angry energy and promote calm, clear communication.

- Add yarrow to your workings with other magickal herbs to enhance their power.

Yarrow Projects

Pine (*Pinus* spp.)

FOLK NAMES: Before the nineteenth century, pines were often called firs, which comes from the Old Norse *fura*. **Note:** Pines and firs are two different species.

FAMILY: Pinaceae

ASTROLOGY: Mars, Pisces

ELEMENT: Air

PLANT LORE: The pine is sacred to many cultures across the globe. Ancient Romans ate pine nuts to increase their energy and stamina. Ancient Greeks burned pine resin as incense to purify their sacred temples and as a symbol of eternal life. Pine is sacred to Poseidon, Greek god of the sea and storms. Greeks used pine pitch (sap) to caulk their boats to protect them on the sea. Pines are sacred to the Celts and Druids. Druids referred to this tree as the "sweetest of the woods," and considered it to be a motherly symbol of protection, longevity, and immortality. Native American people have historically viewed this evergreen (always green) tree as a symbol of longevity, wisdom, peace, and harmony with nature. This sacred tree is woven into their stories, one being *The First Pine Trees*, a legend of the Mi'kmaq people.

MAGICKAL CORRESPONDENCES: health and healing, vitality, immortality, fertility, wisdom, money, love, joy, cleansing negative energies, protection, Yule (Winter Solstice), renewal and beginnings, forgiveness

Identification

Pines are evergreen, coniferous, resinous trees (some shrubs) from the Pinus genus, which contains more than 120 species. They bear pinecones and have bundles of aromatic needles that grow in spirals. Conifers are believed to have evolved approximately 300 million years ago. Pines prefer poor acidic and sandy soil but can tolerate wetter soil. They are native to the Northern Hemisphere and some tropical parts of the Southern Hemisphere. Many common species of pine are used as landscaping trees and shrubs, so you might not have to look any further than just beyond your front door. The young tips of spring provide the most medicine, while autumn needles are more resinous. The inner bark is edible. You can extract it from the trunk of the pine if you know what you're doing, but only from a very small area, so the tree can heal quickly. **Note:** It is illegal to harvest the inner bark of pine trees in national forests.

PARTS USED: needles (which are technically leaves), seeds (pine nuts), and inner bark

Fallen Branches

After a storm, I look for newly fallen pine branches or I do some mindful pruning of branches that encroach upon our driveway. I gather pine sap from Eastern White Pines that grow on our property and burn tiny amounts at Yule or whenever I wish to cleanse the energy in our home and enjoy the refreshing, woodsy scent.

Medicinal and Culinary Uses

Pine calms the nerves, lifts the mood, and provides clarity of mind. It contains antioxidants that fight free radical damage. Pine can break up phlegm in the chest. Pine needles are a powerful source of vitamin C and taste piney, sometimes with a citrusy note.

- Chew on raw needles to extract their nutrients or make a tea by brewing a small handful in 1 cup (235 ml) of boiling water for 10 to 15 minutes.

- Make a pine needle–infused apple cider vinegar for culinary purposes, or mix in some honey to create an ancient medicinal herbal preparation called an oxymel (page 119).

- To quiet a cough, try a pine needle–infused syrup or honey (page 115, variation, and page 123, variation).

- Create a pine needle salve (page 138, variation) or infused body oil (page 131) to increase circulation and ease muscle and nerve pain.

- Use pine as a natural cleansing agent to make a home cleaning product (page 181).

- Strip the outer bark with a knife to get to the inner bark. Cook the inner bark strips in a skillet with your favorite oil. Sprinkle with salt and season as you please. It makes a delightful, healthy, crunchy snack.

Pine Nuts

The seeds, also called pine nuts, are edible. Pine nuts that you buy in the grocery store come from the Pinyon Pine, as they produce the largest seeds. Extracting them from pinecones is labor-intensive and sticky work. If you ever need to get pitch off your hands, use peanut butter.

Magickal Uses

Pine is historically used to help get over feelings of guilt, especially in the context of something that was not your fault. It helps in letting go and finding forgiveness for yourself.

I'll often burn pinches of dried pine needles with dried sage and mint to increase its cleansing power. You can buy special charcoal discs meant for burning incense on (not the same as grill charcoal). Be sure to use a heatproof vessel and follow the instructions on page 167.

- Burn pine resin (sap) as an incense to celebrate the returning of light at Winter Solstice (Yule).

- Follow in the Celtic tradition of casting circles of protection made from pinecones. I have a circular table where I conduct my divination, spellwork, and spirit communication practices. I gather pinecones from the woods and place them around the perimeter of the table, replicating this ancient practice.

- Fill a muslin drawstring bag with fresh pinecones, needles, and bark, and submerge it in your ritual bath for increased circulation, and feelings of calm, peace, and invigoration. I call it my joy bath!

- Gather pine boughs and pinecones from the woods and weave them into a lovely garland of forgiveness.

- Use pine to help you befriend and connect with the nature spirits of the woods. You can reach out to them and ask for assistance on your foraging adventures. Don't forget to reciprocate with an offering of thanks.

- Wrap pine needles in green ribbon, and as you do, envision a new project or existing project that you would like to bring to fruition. Keep this talisman as a reminder and a charm for helping you realize your dreams.

Pine Projects

Pine Oxymel with Wild Apple Cider Vinegar (page 117)

Peppermint-Infused Medicinal Honey (variation, page 123)

Dandelion and Plantain All-Purpose Healing Salve (variation, page 138)

Woodland Whipped Body Butter (page 143)

Spell Jars (page 159)

Intentional Tea Blends (page 161)

Candle Dressing (page 163)

Herbal and Resin Incense (page 167)

Smoke-Cleansing Bouquet (page 170)

Wheel of the Year Ritual Baths (page 173)

Black Salt (page 175)

Cauldron Simmering Potpourri (page 177)

Wildcrafted Witch's Broom (page 183)

Crystal and Herb Grid Magick (page 185)

Apple (*Malus* spp.)

FOLK NAMES: Tree of Love, Silver Branch, The Silver Bough

FAMILY: Rosaceae

ASTROLOGY: Venus, Taurus

ELEMENT: Water

PLANT LORE: Ancient Greeks viewed the apple as a symbol of wisdom and as a fruit that grew on a tree of life in the gardens of the Hesperides. The apple is associated with Greek goddess Aphrodite and Roman goddess Diana (whose equivalent is Artemis). August 13 marks the ancient festival day for Diana, where apples (which are sacred to her) have traditionally been displayed on their boughs. The apple tree is revered by Celts and Druids as a holy tree and woven into their myths, legends, and folklore. They knew the secret that the apple held—that within it, the seeds formed a perfect pentagram representing Earth, Air, Fire, and Water, bound by Spirit. The apple has a strong connection to the sabbat Samhain, as it is considered the "food of the dead." Samhain is often called the "Feast of Apples." Many Halloween legends are associated with the apple. Some say that if you bury an apple in the ground beneath the light of a Halloween moon, it will provide nourishment and healing for the souls of the dead who wander the Earth on this mystical night. Apple growers would bury thirteen leaves from an apple tree in their orchard on Halloween, in complete silence and in secret, to ensure a hardy future crop. Unicorns are said to live beneath apple trees and can be spotted gallivanting in orchards on silvery, foggy mornings.

MAGICKAL CORRESPONDENCES: love, healing, longevity, immortality, Elemental magick, Samhain, divination, spirit communication, blessings, feminine energy, life after death, knowledge and wisdom, magick within

Identification

Apple trees are native to temperate climates in the Northern Hemisphere, cultivated all around the world, and come in 7,500 varieties. There are nearly fifty-five Malus species in the Rosaceae family, both domesticated orchard apples (also known as culinary apples), and wild apples (my favorite) that grow on old farmland and in abandoned orchards. I'm blessed to be granted permission by neighbors in my small Maine town to harvest their wild apples in the fall. Wild apples look like their cultivated relatives but are usually smaller and asymmetrical and have blemishes and bruises. No matter, as those damaged spots can be cut away and the remaining parts can be used for all kinds of recipes. Wild apples are usually not pleasant for consuming raw, but for cooking and baking they are superb.

PARTS USED: fruit (apple), blossoms, leaves, bark

Medicinal and Culinary Uses

Food is medicine. Apples are rich in vitamins and minerals. They improve circulation, support the functions of the nervous system and brain, are high in fiber, beneficial to the liver, good for easing heartburn and upset stomach, and make an ideal

healthy snack that releases its natural sugars slowly, keeping blood sugar stable. I have experimented with wild apples from many trees and use them to make a variety of culinary treats. The tartier ones (including crab apples) have a higher pectin content, so work well for jams and jellies and can be combined with sweeter, low-pectin fruits for flavoring (my favorite being strawberries).

- Turn the unsprayed blossoms into glycerites (page 130, variation) and infused medicinal honeys (page 123, variation). They soothe a sore throat and can be used as a cold preventive.

- Use apple cider vinegar to make fire cider for immune support. Fire cider is actually an oxymel with a variety of immune system-supporting herbs added to it. In my fire cider, I use garlic, onion, ginger, turmeric, horseradish root, rosemary, oregano, thyme, rose hip, goldenrod, hot peppers, lemon peel, and cayenne powder (page 117).

- Dilute apple cider vinegar with water for a facial toner to help clear and prevent acne: Use ½ to 2 tablespoons (8 to 30 ml) to 1 cup (235 ml) of water. You can also use it to soothe sunburn, take the itch out of a bug bite, or as a hair rinse to clarify hair and treat dandruff. You can even spritz some on as a deodorant.

- Use tartier apples to make fantastic wild cider, apple cider vinegar (page 117), and apple wine. Use the sweeter ones for dehydrated apple snacks, pies, crisps, cobblers, apple butter, apple sauce, and chutney.

- Stew apples and pour them over your morning oatmeal.

- Use sweet and tart apples to make a tasty fruit leather. Start by making a puree with peeled and chopped apple, water, sugar, and cinnamon. Spread the puree on a baking sheet lined with a silicone baking mat and place it in a dehydrator, near a wood stove, or in the oven as low as it will go for 2 to 3 hours so that the puree dries out.

Magickal Uses

Apple love divination has a long history you can draw from. Dried seeds, dried blossoms, and ground bark can strengthen divination, spirit communication, and Elemental magick. Apples have long been used for love spells. The wood of a fallen apple branch can be used to craft magickal tools. (I generally do not take branches from live trees, unless I am pruning them.) Apple is the wood traditionally used for the witch's wand and viewed as having strong, magickal powers.

- Burn apple incense (page 167) to provide an energy boost to your spiritual workings.

- Collect some apple blossoms, dry them, grind them up and use them with a heat-safe anointing oil to dress a candle (page 163), burning the candle with the intention of enhancing a current love or calling a future mate to you. Envision growing love for an existing relationship or concentrate on the traits you wish to have in a mate if you are calling one to you.

- To see a vision of your future partner on Halloween night, turn out the lights, light a candle, cut an apple into nine pieces, and eat eight of them while gazing in the mirror. Pierce the ninth piece with your paring knife and hold it over your shoulder. The apparition of your future partner is said to appear to you and take it.

- To make a wand, find a small apple branch that calls to you and whittle it with a knife, if you wish, to achieve a smooth texture. Seal your wand with melted beeswax to protect the wood. You may wish to decorate it with crystals and charms or leave it natural (perfect for the green witch).

- Use found fallen apple wood to create a set of runes which can be used for divining information via casting layouts and spreads (much like tarot). Small branches are perfect for making a set of circular runes. Simply paint the rune symbols onto the branch slices, or use a wood burning tool to burn them into the wood. You can easily learn more about rune symbols, their meanings, and how to use a set of runes by doing a search for "Elder Futhark runes," which is the oldest form of runic alphabets.

Apple Projects

Pine Oxymel with Wild Apple Cider Vinegar (page 117)

Peppermint-Infused Medicinal Honey (variation, page 123)

Lavender Glycerite (variation, page 130)

Dandelion and Plantain All-Purpose Healing Salve (variation, page 138)

Vanilla Chocolate Mint Lip Balm (variation, page 141)

Spell Jars (page 159)

Intentional Tea Blends (page 161)

Candle Dressing (page 163)

Herbal and Resin Incense (variation, page 167)

Smoke-Cleansing Bouquet (page 170)

Wheel of the Year Ritual Baths (page 173)

Cauldron Simmering Potpourri (page 177)

Magickal Mist (page 181)

Wildcrafted Witch's Broom (page 183)

PART III

....

Herbal Remedies, Recipes,
and Magickal Workings

Now that we've gotten to know (remember) thirteen sacred, essential plants for the witch's cupboard for their medicinal, culinary, and magickal uses, it's time to roll up our sleeves and get to the making and the doing. First, to ensure success with the plant-based creations you'll be crafting in the chapters to come, we'll talk about some of the basics of gardening, foraging, and herbalism.

As you learn more about bringing herbs into your life and magickal practice, I encourage you to review the plant cautions (page 9) and revisit the detailed descriptions in the plant profiles for the plant or plants that you work with in each project. A field guide specific to your region is a must if you're doing any foraging. The projects in chapters 7 and 8 will apply your knowledge in an authentic, hands-on way. We'll make natural remedies, recipes, and magickal creations that can support your health, well-being, and magickal pursuits. Have fun!

CHAPTER 6

Gardening, Foraging, and Herbalism Basics

G ardening, foraging, and herbalism provide hands-on experiences that invite you to deeply connect with nature, with your green witch ancestors, and with your body and your soul. These are sensual and spiritual endeavors in which you feel and smell the earth beneath your feet and in your hands. You nurture and witness the growth of plants from little seedlings to full-grown beautiful, green creatures. You appreciate and receive their healing and nourishing bountiful gifts of food and medicine.

When we work with green energy in this manner, our entire being becomes fully engaged and our mind quiets. We become open to listening to the teachings of Mother Nature. We learn about plants' energies, the rhythms of the seasons, and the natural cycle of life—birth, death, and rebirth.

Green Witch Gardening

It is possible to garden wherever you are, even if you live in an urban setting where space is limited. Let's take a brief look at three possibilities for growing your green witch garden, and then get into some aspects of care. See which option or options are a good fit for you, considering your living space, lifestyle, and amount of time you can devote to gardening.

Container Gardening

This is a great place to start if you are new to gardening. It's how I started more than twenty years ago, with a window box of kitchen herbs in my little studio apartment in Boston. Depending on your living space, you can use window boxes on windowsills, place containers in sunny windows, or on your porch, patio, or balcony.

Yes, gardening does require monetary investment, but I'm the queen of finding ways to do it on the cheap—thrifty ways that are actually eco-friendly, beneficial to the environment, and support local businesses and charitable endeavors. My best piece of advice is to buy local, whenever possible, for your soil, plants, seeds, and containers. Avoid the big chain garden centers if you can, and instead hit up your local nurseries, farmers' markets, and farm stands. Look for plant sales held by community organizations such as libraries. They're a great way to get inexpensive plants, support a good cause, and socially connect with other gardeners who are happy to lend advice and help.

For container gardening, the easy-to-care-for, hardy kitchen herbs in chapter 3 are ideal, as are oregano, thyme, chamomile, chives, dill, cilantro, parsley, calendula, and yarrow. If you're a beginner, I recommend purchasing seedlings (baby plants), as opposed to starting plants from seed, as that process can be somewhat involved. Purchase a nutrient-rich, organic potting soil for your containers (not regular garden soil). For plants that require a little more drainage, such as rosemary, you can line the bottom of your pot with some stones to promote better drainage.

DIY Raised Beds

You can make your own raised beds or have them custom-built. You can find kits at a local gardening center or hardware store, or you can create your own. Look for designs that use what you have available and will work for your space and needs. Raised beds can be constructed from pavers, found rocks, wooden pallets, galvanized water troughs (with holes drilled for drainage), straw bales (avoid hay, as it reseeds), or even thick-cut logs from fallen hardwood trees (which I've done). Explore the possibilities!

Reuse, recycle, and have fun thrifting when on your quest for plant containers. You can find terracotta and artistic pottery plant pots of all sizes (with draining holes and pot saucers) at yard sales, thrift stores, and town recycling centers. When I lived in the city, I often found them left curbside for the taking, along with some awesome funky furniture. I recommend setting up your containers so that they are raised and do not come in contact with the surface below, especially with wooden surfaces, to prevent moisture damage. You might be able to thrift some plant stands, or you can repurpose tiles, thick woven mats, coasters, or hot plates.

Raised Beds and Small Plots

Raised beds are sometimes a preferable way to garden, especially if the soil beneath is not ideal. This method also helps in containing plants, keeps a lot of the weeds out, and allows you to create an organized, aesthetically pleasing, and functional design. If you are a city dweller, look into obtaining a plot at a community garden. Raised beds are perfect for vegetables and plants that don't sprawl or take over, such as rosemary, basil, sage, lavender, chamomile, calendula, echinacea, lemon balm, St. John's wort, thyme, yarrow, and tulsi.

Helpful Plant Care Tips for Any Garden

- Mulching is important, especially for small plots, as it helps the plants retain moisture after watering.

- Water your plants at their bases either in the early morning or evening, for best absorption, less evaporation, and to prevent leaf issues such as powdery mildew. A general rule of thumb for an amount is 1 inch (2.5 cm) of water per week (from devices and rain).

- For outdoor container gardens in full sun, give them a good drink every other day, if it does not rain. Plants will let you know if they need water, through obvious signs such as wilting. Indoor plants in a sunny window generally need to be watered about once a week.

- Check on outdoor plants daily, especially ones in raised beds and small plots that are more vulnerable. Pests can take over quickly. Pest problems can be remedied naturally, without chemicals. There are plenty of online resources. For me, pennies are a must for protecting against slugs; they are repelled by copper.

- Pull off yellowed leaves and deadhead spent flowers (removing dead flowers) so the energy of the plant can go to creating new growth. **Note:** You can leave some flower heads if you wish, for the plant to reseed itself.

Small plots are another option for gardeners. They can be dedicated vegetable and herb garden plots, or plots used to beautify your landscape. I have eight small plots, in addition to eight raised beds, and a variety of container gardens on my porch, patio, and deck. My small plots are located throughout our property, contain primarily established flowering ornamentals to beautify the landscape, but also edible and medicinal plants that I've woven in. They provide food and medicine, and they add color and texture to my garden. They also attract pollinators and serve as beneficial companion plants. I like to include echinacea, yarrow, valerian, calendula, marshmallow, elecampane, thyme, anise hyssop, bee balm, black cohosh, nasturtium, lady's mantle, spilanthes, borage, and beach rose (Rosa rugosa).

Plant Care

Good, organic soil is key to successful gardening. Nutrient-rich potting soil is ideal for containers, and you should replace or refresh potting soil yearly. I'll give my potted plants organic plant food only during their active growing phases (in warmer months), about twice during that time. Raised beds and small plots require garden soil, and it should be fertilized with organic matter every year. A Master Gardener once told me that ideal times for fertilizing during the growing season are early spring and then again just before July 4. Dehydrated cow manure is my compost of choice. I also like to occasionally sprinkle wood stove ash, coffee grinds, grass clippings, or leaves onto the soil to provide necessary nutrients such as potassium, nitrogen, and magnesium.

If your soil contains lots of earthworms, that's an indicator of it being fertile. On the other hand, if you're having trouble with your soil, you can send a sample of it to your state's soil testing laboratory for a thorough analysis and recommendations for amendments.

Remember that balance is important. Don't overdo or underdo plant care. Be careful not to water too much or too little. Soil should generally feel moist but not soggy. When it feels hard and dry, it's time to water. The soil should be healthy, not depleted or overly rich.

It also helps to keep a garden journal: Note what worked, what didn't, and jot down garden plans and dreams. Remember that gardening is an ever-changing and ever-evolving process that can differ from year to year, depending on many variables. Even the most experienced gardeners and farmers encounter challenges. They have good years when yield is plentiful and bad years due to things such as blight, lack of rain, too much rain, or cold weather. It's all a part of this natural process.

Foraging Basics

Foraging attracts people who are interested in incorporating wild food into their diets. Wild foods are packed with vitamins and minerals and have higher amounts of nutrients than farmed produce grown in soil that has been depleted over the years by over-farming. Other people are drawn to foraging because they are intrigued by new tastes that they can't find in the grocery store. It's free food, and for so many people experiencing food insecurity, this is a way to address that. Foraging makes for a fun treasure hunt, and I'll admit it is a rather addictive activity.

Many green witches forage for safe, healing plants to be used in culinary recipes and in herbal remedies. They also gather wild plants for their spellwork, rituals, and divination practices, all with the intent to serve and bring about positive change, balance, and harmony.

Essential Tools and Supplies

Before heading out into the field with enthusiasm, it's important to have tools at your disposal. If you're going into the woods or a field with tall grass, wear long pants and long sleeves, tuck your pants into your socks, and wear comfortable hiking shoes.

Wearing an insect/tick repellent is a must. Be sure to check yourself for ticks afterward, if ticks are a problem in your area. I wear light clothing without patterns, as it's much easier to see ticks on these surfaces. If it's hunting season in your area, wear fluorescent orange.

Bring a foraging tote, guidebooks, a compass, lunch-sized paper bags for holding your harvests, scissors, and an outdoor folding knife. If you're carrying a phone, wrap its case in fluorescent orange, as it will be much easier to find if you lose it in the woods. (Yup, it has happened to me.)

Safety

- Make sure you can 100 percent positively identify a plant before using it for culinary or medicinal purposes. When you're starting, I highly recommend taking a local foraging class from an experienced forager. Also, make sure to cross-check many guidebooks.

- Once you have made a positive identification, try only a tiny portion to see if the plant agrees with you.

- Do not forage in suburban areas, near golf courses, or near industrial agricultural farms. You will encounter polluted plants riddled with pesticides and heavy metals. If you live in a city or suburban area, look for edible and medicinal wild plants popping up alongside vegetables in your community gardens. Those should be safe to use, as long as the soil has been tested and is safe.

- The rule of thumb for harvesting near busy roads is 50 feet (15.2 m) away. If you are downhill from the road, 100 feet (30.5 m) away is safe. Uphill, you can be closer than 50 feet.

Laws

- Do not forage on private property unless you have permission. If you are granted permission, it is always nice to gift the landowner with a portion of your harvest, or something you made from the harvest.

- Don't assume that you can forage in a state or national park. Some parks forbid it; others have quotas.

- Some community parks do allow foraging; check the rules and ask about possible pesticide spraying before foraging.

Ethics

- Harvest with gratitude only what you need, and use everything that you harvest.

- Share.

- Do not forage endangered plants.

- With invasive, nonnative species the "amount" rule is different. For example, plantain and mugwort are both nonnative, invasive plants in North America that can choke out other plants. You can safely take more of these plants, as it helps the environment by making room for native plants.

Honorable Harvest

The Haudenosaunee—a historical indigenous confederacy among five Native American nations (the Mohawks, Oneidas, Onondagas, Cayugas, and Senecas)—give the following guidelines: You must ask the plant for permission before taking it, and abide by the answer. Do not take the first or the last. Never take more than half and leave some for others. Give a gift in return for what you have taken. "Sustain the ones who sustain you and the Earth will last forever."

Herbalism Basics

The herbalism explored in this book is considered "folk" or "family" herbalism, which is a pragmatic, home-remedy form of herbalism (as opposed to clinical herbalism) that focuses on nonemergency health support. This form of herbalism uses safe plant allies, many of which we already grow in our gardens and use in our home kitchens.

Note: Remember that the word *safe* is a somewhat relative term. There are plenty of "safe" foods in the grocery store that give some people allergic reactions. Family herbalism is no different, so always proceed with caution.

Essential Tools and Supplies

You'll need containers for storing dried herbs, infused oils, salves, and tinctures. I recommend:

- pint and quart-sized mason jars (light-blocking amber glass is a plus for preservation)
- 1- or 2-ounce (30 or 60 ml) Boston round glass bottles with droppers
- 1- or 2-ounce (30 or 60 ml) salve tins
- Smaller tins for lip balms

You can get thrifty and reuse food containers, or purchase supplies at second-hand stores and yard sales. Just thoroughly clean and sterilize them.

You'll also need:

- A spray bottle filled with 190 proof alcohol, for sterilizing containers and utensils. (I do not recommend using rubbing alcohol, as its fumes are unsafe for the lungs.)
- Fine-mesh strainers in various sizes
- Cheesecloth for straining out fine plant matter
- Stainless-steel or glass pots (no aluminum)
- A double boiler (I use either a recycled, cleaned, BPA-free soup can or Pyrex measuring cup and a stainless-steel pot.)
- A kitchen digital scale
- A coffee grinder reserved for grinding herbs
- A handheld or stand mixer (for making whipped body butters)

Harvesting

You'll want to harvest plants when they can offer you the most medicine. In general, it is best to harvest leaves before a plant reaches full bloom. There are exceptions, such as mint, which is most potent when it is flowering. For flowers, harvest them when they begin to open, as opposed to waiting until they are in full bloom. Roots contain the highest amounts of medicine in the fall, just after the first frost, and in early spring before the plant's energy moves upward to support its aerial growth.

Processing

Herbs can be used fresh (or fresh-wilted for making oil-based remedies, to release some of the initial moisture). You can also preserve herbs for later use through freezing or drying. Freezing preserves vitamins and minerals, and thawed plant matter works well for culinary purposes and for some medicinal remedies.

There are several ways to dry plants. Ideally, they should be dried in a dark, dry place with good airflow and minimal moisture. I dry a lot of my herbs on screens, in large baskets, and I hang them in small bundles in dark closets and in dark rooms. The process generally takes 2 to 4 weeks, depending on the plant and the environment. Sometimes I'll use my dehydrator, but mostly for roots, fruits, and mushrooms.

As soon as the plant matter is dried, I place it in an airtight container. I do not chop the plants until I use them in herbal preparations, as they will last longer if kept intact. I use amber-tinted mason jars and clear ones with homemade light-protective sleeves, as both light and oxygen can degrade the potency of herbs. When preserved properly, your plant matter should stay fresh for about one year.

Types of Herbal Remedies

HERB-INFUSED OIL: A skin-friendly carrier oil that is infused with either fresh-wilted or dried plant matter.

SALVES, BALMS, AND OINTMENTS: A blend of herb-infused oil and wax (usually beeswax). The beeswax provides the solid texture and contains skin-healing constituents. A balm contains more wax than a salve, giving it a firmer texture. An ointment is a softer salve with less wax.

TINCTURE (EXTRACT): A highly concentrated herbal formulation of fresh or dried herbs plus alcohol, apple cider vinegar, or vegetable glycerine. Alcohol is the most potent solvent for extraction and should be 80 to 100 proof. (I prefer 100 proof vodka; some folks like to use brandy, rum, or gin.)

GLYCERITE (GLYCERIN-BASED TINCTURE): Made of 100 percent vegetable glycerin plus fresh or dried herbs. If dried herbs are used, some water is added to the preparation. These are ideal for children and people who would like to use a tincture without the alcohol content.

OXYMEL: A medicinal formulation made of plant matter, apple cider vinegar, and raw honey. Traditionally used for treating coughs and colds and to support the immune system.

CHAPTER 7

Herbal Remedies
and Recipes

I t's time to apply our knowledge of these beloved plant
friends to hands-on herbal remedies and recipes. Working
with plants is a give-and-take relationship. It is a tangible and
spiritual way to learn that by giving, we receive. We become
forever changed when working with green energy in this
connected way, arriving at a place where we wish to give back
to the Earth more than we have taken, leaving Her better than
we found Her, helping to restore balance and harmony to the
planet and ourselves.

I believe this is where the true learning takes place—in the
making and the doing—co-creating with these amazing,
healing plants to make nourishing food and medicine that
can support our health and well-being.

Wild Greens Pesto

Every year, I make batches of wild greens pesto for my family. I also freeze it in jam jars to enjoy throughout the long, long Maine winter. There's something magickal and warming about experiencing the flavors and aromas of summer's wild greens on a snowy December day. With every bite, part of me stays connected to the height and vibrancy of summer—such a precious gift in the dark, cold winter.

My wild greens of choice for this recipe are dandelion leaves and plantain leaves. Be sure to use smaller leaves. I combine them with basil leaves, along with nasturtium leaves and blossoms for a peppery, spicy taste. Try making this with a bit of oregano, garlic chives, wild violet leaves (*Viola odorata*), stinging nettle leaves, purslane, and lamb's-quarter (wild spinach).

CAUTION: Please review plant cautions on page 9 and do your research to ensure safe use. If using stinging nettle, handle with gloves and boil for 1 minute to remove the sting, then squeeze to remove the water.

Makes about five 4-ounce (120-ml) jam jars

1 cup (55 g) small dandelion leaves, plantain leaves, basil, and any other greens you'd like to include

⅓ cup (27 g) grated Parmesan cheese

⅓ cup (40 g) walnuts, pine nuts, or pumpkin seeds

½ cup (120 ml) olive oil

2 to 3 chopped garlic cloves or garlic chives

1 to 2 tablespoons (15 to 20 ml) fresh lemon juice or a few dashes of lemon pepper

Salt and pepper

Put all the ingredients in a food processor. Blend thoroughly, stopping to scrape down the sides as needed. Pour into 4-ounce (120-ml) jam jars, leaving a little headspace for freezing expansion. Store the capped jars in the fridge for 1 week or in the freezer for up to 1 year. Enjoy with pasta, over eggs, as a sandwich condiment, on chicken, baked into bread, mixed into salad dressing, as a bean burrito topping, and more.

notes

- Make a larger batch for freezing. I quadruple the recipe; it's the maximum amount my food processor can fit. I try to make at least six batches a year to freeze.

- You can substitute budget-friendly pumpkin seeds for some or all of the nuts. I also like to sprinkle in some sesame seeds.

Rose Petal Simple Syrup

In early summer, I spend time with my head in the blooming wild beach roses that grow all along the Maine coast. Their rosy floral, citrusy fragrance combined with the salty air of the ocean is intoxicating and otherworldly. I celebrate their return by relaxing in a rose petal ritual milk bath and infusing some in oils for herbal concoctions. I also make rose petal simple syrup—the perfect addition to summertime cocktails, lemonade, soda water, champagne, or vanilla ice cream.

Use any rose petals, as long as they are unsprayed and not from a florist. I recommend making this syrup with a neutral honey, such as clover, so the herb flavors come through. If you're using the syrup in a cocktail, you may wish to go with sugar. It's all a matter of personal choice and taste.

CAUTION: Please review plant cautions on page 9 and do your research to ensure safe use.

Makes 1½ cups (355 ml)

½ cup (120 ml) honey or 1 cup (200 g) pure cane sugar
1 cup (235 ml) water

1 cup (16 g) fresh rose petals or ½ cup (15 g) dried

Dissolve the honey in water in a small saucepan over a low heat. Add the rose petals and simmer for 10 minutes. Remove from the heat and allow to steep for 20 minutes. Strain out rose petals through a fine-mesh strainer. Allow to cool. Store in the refrigerator for up to 1 month.

VARIATIONS

LAVENDER SIMPLE SYRUP: Use 2 tablespoons (5.5 g) of fresh lavender or 1½ (5 g) tablespoons dried instead of the rose petals. This is delicious when added to lemonade or drizzled over lemon sorbet. I like it in my coffee with cream.

ROSEMARY SIMPLE SYRUP: Use ¼ cup (7 g) of chopped fresh rosemary or thawed frozen rosemary instead of the rose petals.

MINT SIMPLE SYRUP: Use 1 cup (14 g) fresh mint instead of rose petals. Mint syrup is delicious over chocolate ice cream (like an Andes chocolate mint candy).

(continued)

notes

- Use the honey-based rose syrup as a cough remedy. Rosemary and mint syrups are also good for colds.

- Vegans commonly substitute 100 percent vegetable glycerin or coconut sugar for the honey.

Lemon Rose Drop

Makes 1 serving

Coat the edge of a chilled martini glass with a lemon wedge. Dip or roll it in a plate of sugar to create a sugared rim. Combine 2 ounces (60 ml) of vodka, ¾ ounce (22 ml) of fresh lemon juice, and ¾ ounce (22 ml) of rose petal simple syrup in a cocktail shaker with ice. Shake until cold and strain into the glass. Garnish with a rose petal or two.

Rosemary Gimlet

Makes 1 serving

Combine 2 ounces (60 ml) of gin, ¾ ounce (22 ml) of fresh lime juice, and ¾ ounce (22 ml) of rosemary syrup in a cocktail shaker with ice. Shake until cold. Strain into a chilled cocktail glass. Garnish with a sprig of rosemary.

Easy and Refreshing Mojito

Makes 1 serving

Combine 2 ounces (60 ml) of light rum, ¾ ounce (22 ml) of fresh lime juice, and ¾ ounce (22 ml) of mint syrup in a cocktail shaker with ice. Shake until cold. Strain/pour over the rocks. Top with club soda. Garnish with a mint leaf.

Pine Oxymel with Wild Apple Cider Vinegar

An oxymel is a medicinal preparation that combines vinegar and honey, and it has been used since ancient times to support respiratory and immune systems. Today, people like to make oxymels with apple cider vinegar and medicinal herbs to boost the healing power of this tonic. The popular "fire cider" is based on the classic oxymel.

CAUTION: Please review plant cautions on page 9 and do your research to ensure safe use.

Wild Apple Cider Vinegar

Crafting your own apple cider vinegar is easier than you may think and works especially well with tartier wild apples. (Store-bought ones will work just fine.) Any part of the apple, including the skin and core, and any bruised parts, can be used. Just chop them up into smaller pieces first.

Makes about 24 ounces (710 ml)

Fill a quart-sized (1-L) mason jar three-quarters full with chopped apple pieces. Dissolve 2 tablespoons (26 g) of pure cane sugar in 2 cups (470 ml) of room temperature filtered water. Pour this mixture over the apples until they are completely covered, adding more filtered water if necessary.

Keep the apples from floating to the top either with a special weight used for fermenting and pickling or with a small glass jar: You don't want the fruit exposed to the air, introducing the possibility of mold. Put the weight in place and cover your jar with a coffee filter or cheesecloth and secure it with a rubber band.

Store the jar in your kitchen cabinet or dark corner on your kitchen counter for 2 weeks. Check now and then to ensure that the apples are fully submerged. Bubbles will form as the sugar ferments, and you will smell it happening.

At the 2-week mark, strain out the apples and return the apple cider vinegar to the jar. Cover it again with a fresh cover and place it in your dark space for another 2 to 4 weeks, stirring it periodically.

At 2 weeks, give it a taste. When your apple cider vinegar has reached a desired flavor, it's ready for use. If you accidentally let it go too long, and it gets too strong, pour some of it out and replace it with fresh filtered water.

Store it in the jar and capped with a nonreactive lid, or transfer it to a bottle. I like to save the "mother"—the cloudy looking culture of beneficial bacteria that transforms the juice into vinegar—and a small bit of apple cider vinegar to start a new batch with. It speeds up the fermentation process.

(continued)

note

Vegans substitute maple syrup, rice malt syrup, or agave nectar for honey. (There are ethical issues around the harvesting of agave nectar, so please do your research.) These vegan substitutes do not have the natural preservation capability that honey does, so be sure to refrigerate this product and consume it swiftly.

An appropriate serving amount is 1 tablespoon. You can drink it neat or dilute it in hot water. Use it as a flavoring in a soda water (my favorite), as an addition to a cocktail, or even as a salad dressing or marinade.

Pine Oxymel

There are a few different approaches for crafting herbal oxymels. You can use fresh or dried herb. I prefer working with fresh plants, as nutrient content becomes reduced when a harvested plant is dried.

CAUTION: Please review plant cautions on page 9 and do your research to ensure safe use.

Makes about 2¾ cups (828 ml)

> Fresh pine needles (You'll need enough fresh needles to fill a pint-sized, or 473-ml, jar. If using dried herb, you'll only need to fill the jar halfway.)
> Apple cider vinegar
> ¾ cup (175 ml) raw honey or to taste

Chop the pine needles coarsely and place them in a pint-size mason jar. Pour apple cider vinegar over the plant matter, all the way to the top. Stir to release the air bubbles and to fully combine the ingredients. Cover with a nonreactive lid or put a piece of waxed paper under the metal mason jar lid.

Allow the oxymel to brew for 4 to 6 weeks in a cool and dark place, shaking it daily. Check it on day 2 and add more apple cider vinegar if you need to, to fill it to the top, as the plant material will absorb it. Don't leave any room for air, which can lead to oxidation and spoilage.

After the 4 to 6 weeks, strain out the pine needles. Combine the liquid with the honey in a clean jar or bottle. Cover with a nonreactive lid, label it, and store in the refrigerator for up to 1 year.

VARIATIONS

Other herbs to incorporate in your oxymels include:

- basil
- chickweed
- dandelion
- elderflowers or fully ripe elderberries (Green, unripe elderberries are poisonous.)
- garlic
- lemon balm
- nettle (Use dried.)
- oregano
- red clover
- rose petals
- rosemary (Dried is fine.)
- sage
- thyme
- violet blossoms

Clover Blossom Banana Bread

We have an abundance of fragrant white clover that covers our lawn in summertime, providing our family with nutritious food and medicine. White clover makes a wonderful ground cover, provides for the bees, and feeds the soil with nitrogen. For this banana bread recipe, you can opt to grind fully dried blossoms into a "flour" (a coffee grinder works well for this purpose), or you can use them whole. I like to use the whole blossoms for this recipe, as they add a pleasing texture and visual appeal. Just pull apart the blossom heads into individual florets. This healthy clover banana bread is free of grains and sugar and packed with nutrients. It's an excellent source of protein and will give you long-lasting energy.

CAUTION: Please review plant cautions on page 9 and do your research to ensure safe use.

Makes 1 loaf

3 overly ripe medium-size bananas
3 eggs
⅓ cup (86 g) sunflower butter or other nut butter
¼ cup (60 ml) unsweetened coconut milk
1½ tablespoons (25 ml) melted coconut oil
½ teaspoon vanilla extract
Pinch of salt

1 cup (76 g) dried white and/or red clover blossoms
⅓ cup (50 g) green banana flour
½ teaspoon cinnamon
½ teaspoon baking powder
½ teaspoon baking soda

Preheat oven to 350°F (175°C, or gas mark 4) and lightly coat a loaf pan with coconut oil. I use a 7½ × 3½-inch (19 × 8 cm) pan.

Mash the bananas with either a potato masher or fork. In a large bowl, hand mix bananas, eggs, sunflower butter, coconut milk, coconut oil, vanilla, and salt. In a separate bowl, combine the blossoms, banana flour, cinnamon, baking soda, and baking powder.

Slowly add the flour mixture to wet mixture. Pour evenly into the bread loaf pan and bake about 45 minutes or until golden brown. (I loosely cover mine with tin foil after about 20 minutes, to keep the top from getting too crisp. If you have a larger bread loaf pan, you may need to bake it longer, for about 60 minutes.)

Cool for 10 minutes. Transfer to a wire rack and allow to cool some more. Serve warm with a pat of ghee or butter and a dab of raw honey. It pairs well with roasted dandelion root coffee.

Roasted Dandelion Root Coffee

This coffee substitute is made as a decoction, which is essentially a strong tea—but with no caffeine. Limit to one mug daily, as dandelion is a diuretic.

Makes 1 serving

3 tablespoons (38 g) coarsely ground
   dandelion root
3 cups (705 ml) water
Almond milk (or other milk of choice)

Honey or maple syrup
Pinches of cinnamon, nutmeg, ginger, cardamom,
   and clove, or a dash of vanilla extract

To prepare your dandelion roots for coffee: Follow the harvesting tips in the Dandelion Tincture recipe (page 127). Soak them for a few minutes in water, then scrub them clean with a vegetable brush. Chop them into small pieces.

To roast in a cast-iron pan: Heat the pan over medium-low heat. Add the roots to the pan, stirring and turning them constantly until they take on a dark golden color.

To roast in the oven: Preheat the oven to 350°F (175°C, or gas mark 4). Spread the roots out on a cookie sheet and bake them for 30 minutes, or until the roots take on that deep golden color.

Cool the dandelion roots completely, then grind them up with a coffee grinder.

To make the coffee: Combine the roots with the water. Simmer over low heat for 1 hour. Strain out the roots. Add milk. Sweeten and spice to taste.

Vanilla Rose Moon Milk

Moon milk is an Ayurvedic-style drink that can instill calm and promote a good night's sleep. This warm, comforting preparation contains a dairy or plant-based milk—natural sources of melatonin, magnesium, and tryptophan that help promote sleep. It also includes an adaptogen, which is a plant extract that helps the body adapt to stress and restore its normal functioning.

CAUTION: Please review plant cautions on page 9 and do your research to ensure safe use. Do not exceed the recommended daily dose of your chosen adaptogen.

Makes 1 serving

- 1½ cups (355 ml) milk or almond, cashew, coconut, or oat milk
- 1 teaspoon of adaptogen powder, such as ashwagandha root, reishi, chaga, or astragalus root
- 1 teaspoon spices, such as cinnamon, cardamom, nutmeg, clove, black pepper, gingerroot, and/or turmeric
- 1 teaspoon of sweetener, such as raw honey or maple syrup
- 1 teaspoon of healthy fat, such as ghee, coconut oil, or raw cocoa butter
- 1 teaspoon dried rose petals
- ⅛ teaspoon vanilla extract

Combine all the ingredients in a small saucepan over medium-low heat. Once warmed, pour the milk through a strainer into your mug.

For a frothy finish, you can whisk it or use a frother. (I have a handheld milk frother that I bought for about $12.)

VARIATION

Instead of using dried rose petals, substitute lavender, mint, chamomile, or a blend of these herbs.

note

You can achieve the pretty pink color in several ways. Use a pinch of a supplement powder such as raspberry, tart cherry, or beetroot. Or you can use the juice of a few raspberries or strawberries. Or add 2 tablespoons (30 ml) of homemade beetroot juice. To make beetroot juice, add two slices of beets to a cup of water and simmer for 30 minutes.

Peppermint-Infused Medicinal Honey

Raw honey is a rich and sweet natural treat that offers potent medicine. When infused with medicinal herbs, its healing potential multiplies. Herb-infused honey is easy to make, has a long shelf life, and captures a taste of summer to be enjoyed on a cold winter's day. One of my favorites is peppermint-infused honey, crafted with fresh peppermint from my garden. Wildflower honey tends to overwhelm some of the peppermint flavor, so I choose a more neutral clover honey.

This infused preparation tastes like a candy cane, and I'll admit that I relish eating it by the spoonful throughout the year. It's delightful in tea and makes an effective cough and cold remedy. It soothes sore throats, helps to clear a stuffy nose, supports the immune system, supports the digestive system, calms an upset tummy, and curtails nausea. It's antibacterial, antiviral, and anti-inflammatory.

CAUTION: Please review plant cautions on page 9 and do your research to ensure safe use.

Makes about 2 cups (473 ml) in a pint-sized jar or 4 cups (1 L) in a quart-sized jar

Fresh or dried peppermint   Clover honey

(continued)

---

note

Vegans substitute maple syrup, rice malt syrup, or agave nectar for the honey. These substitutes do not have the natural preservation capability that honey does, so use the slow cooker method and be sure to refrigerate this product and consume it swiftly.

Fill a pint- or quart-size (473-ml or 1-L) mason jar half full with fresh, chopped herb. Fill it one-quarter full if using dried herb (grind the dried herbs first using a mortar and pestle). Pour honey over it, filling the jar all the way to the top. Cap it and set it in a warm spot near a sunny window but out of direct sunlight. Let it sit for 2 weeks.

Strain the infused honey through a cheesecloth-lined strainer and enjoy! Store the honey in a cool, dark pantry or in the refrigerator. It should keep for several months or longer.

Alternatively, you could use a slow cooker set to 100°F (38°C), warming it for several hours. If the temperature goes over 110°F (38°C), it will destroy the honey's beneficial enzymes and medicinal properties. (I've ruined herbal honey this way, so I prefer the slower method.) If you can't set the temperature of your cooker, use a candy or meat thermometer to monitor it. You'll most likely have to turn the cooker off occasionally to reduce the temperature.

VARIATIONS

So many healing plants can be infused into honey. Choose ones with properties that support your medicinal needs.

- Plants from this book: lavender, rose petals, rose hips, apple blossoms, red clover, pine needles, rosemary, sage, basil, mugwort, and plantain (dried only).

- Other plants: bee balm blossoms, tulsi (avoid if pregnant), lemon balm, linden blossoms, elderberry blossoms, thyme, chamomile, and violet blossoms.

Rose Petal Elixir

Elixirs are herbal extracts made of plant matter, honey, and alcohol. If you're making an herb-infused honey, you have the easy option of turning it into an elixir. My favorite elixir, which I make every year, is a rose petal elixir made from beach roses (Rosa rugosa) that I gather from the coast of Maine.

Add the fresh rose petals to a pint- or quart-size (473-ml or 1-L) mason jar. Fill it one-third of the way with honey. Allow it to macerate for a day and then fill the jar to the top with alcohol that is at least 35 percent alcohol content (70 proof). It's unnecessary to use 80 to 100 proof alcohol, as honey has preservative properties, so you can get a little bit fancy here with flavor. I enjoy using a honey liqueur (a tip I learned from herbalist April Graham), and I've also tried a citrus-vanilla one that nicely complements the rose petals.

After filling your jar to the top with the alcohol, cap it and shake it. Allow it to sit for 4 to 6 weeks, shaking it occasionally. Strain out the plant matter through a fine-mesh strainer, and bottle up your elixir. I like filling a dropper bottle for ease of use.

Store in a cool, dark place or in the refrigerator. It should keep for 3 months or longer.

Making Tinctures

A tincture is a highly concentrated herbal preparation that people take internally as a remedy for chronic or acute conditions. Tinctures can also be incorporated into topical remedies. A tincture is made by extracting plant matter with a solvent: alcohol, apple cider vinegar, or 100 percent vegetable glycerin.

The method I use for making alcohol-based tinctures is a simple, traditional, and well-accepted method in the herbalism community, using 80 to 100 proof (40 to 50 percent) alcohol. It's ideal for safe, home-based herbalism. Vodka is used most commonly, but feel free to use brandy, rum, or gin.

I make each tincture in the form of a "simple": one herb only per tincture. I'll blend finished tinctures later, as needed. Simples are especially important if you're new to an herb. Taking one herb at a time allows you to get to know how they feel and how they do their work. If you have a negative reaction, you will know that the herb affected you adversely. If you have amazing results, you will know which plant was responsible.

CAUTION: Tinctures are concentrated herbal extract medicinal preparations. In other words, they are plant medicine. When a plant dries, its volatile oils become more potent and potentially too strong for safe home use. It is important to do your research when tincturing herbs, so you know which ones are safe. Before making an herbal tincture to be taken internally, please review plant cautions on page 9 and do your research to ensure safe use. When trying an herb for the first time, try only a few drops at first, to see how it feels in your body.

Basic Tincture

Makes about 2 cups (473 ml) in a pint-sized jar or 4 cups (1 L) in a quart-sized jar

Fresh herbs (not including rotted or yellowed plant parts) or dried herbs
80 to 100 proof alcohol (I prefer 100 proof vodka.)

Chop fresh plant matter coarsely with a clean pair of scissors. For dried herbs, grind them with a mortar and pestle first, so that they can better release their constituents into the preparation. If tincturing roots, make sure to chop them up well with a knife into small pieces.

Fill a pint- or quart-size (473-ml or 1-L) mason jar with plant matter. I recommend using either a pint or quart-sized mason jar, depending on the amount of tincture you wish to make. Wide-mouth jars are easier to fill with plant matter. For fresh herbs, fill it to the top. For fresh roots, fill the jar halfway. For dry plant matter, fill the jar halfway with your herbs. If tincturing dried roots, fill the jar one-quarter of the way with the roots.

(continued)

Fill the jar to the top with alcohol, completely covering the plant matter. Securely cap and shake the jar. Allow it to sit for 6 to 8 weeks in a dark spot, at room temperature. Label your jar with the name of the plant, type of alcohol used, when you bottled it, and when it will be ready. Shake the jar occasionally.

After a few days, check the alcohol level. You may need to fill it to the top again, as plants absorb the alcohol. After 6 to 8 weeks, strain out the plant matter through a cheesecloth-lined strainer and bottle up your tincture. I like using amber-colored Boston round bottles with droppers, for ease of use. Label them as before. Store in a cool, dark place. Alcohol-based tinctures will generally keep 6 to 8 years, sometimes longer.

Alcohol-based tinctures are often taken with warm water or juice. You can put the drops under the tongue for quicker absorption into the bloodstream. An adult dosage guideline from herbalist Rosemary Gladstar that I personally use:

- Ongoing support of a chronic condition: ½ to 1 teaspoon 2 to 3 times a day, not exceeding 3 teaspoons in a day.
- Acute situation such as a cold or the flu: ¼ to ½ teaspoon up to 6 teaspoons a day, spread out over the course of the day.

My rule of thumb for taking herbs that work well in my body is to take as little as possible to get the desired effect, especially when it comes to supporting a chronic condition. For acute situations, I'll take up to 6 teaspoons a day until I feel better.

Dandelion Tincture

Blessed dandelion is packed with vitamins and minerals. It reduces inflammation in the body and is high in iron. It supports the digestive system and liver and acts as a diuretic, flushing toxins out of the body without depleting potassium. I like to ingest it just before or right after a meal to assist in healthy digestion.

When I make a dandelion tincture, I like to use fresh plant matter and incorporate the entire plant, including the roots. Harvesting roots is best done after the first frost in the fall or in early spring, when the energy of the plant and its potent medicine are contained in its roots (see page 107 for harvesting tips).

CAUTION: Please review plant cautions on page 9 and do your research to ensure safe use.

Makes about 2 cups (473 ml) in a pint-sized jar or 4 cups (1 L) in a quart-sized jar

Dandelion (a combination of fresh aerial parts and roots)
Alcohol
Water, for soaking

To prepare the dandelion: Separate the aerial parts from the roots, using a knife. Do not wash the aerial parts. Soak your roots to loosen dirt and scrub them with a vegetable brush. Pat them dry with a towel. Chop up the aerial parts coarsely. Chop the roots into small pieces.

Fill the jar halfway with roots and then add the aerial parts of the plant, enough to reach the top of the jar. Make the tincture by following the method on page 125 and allow it to steep a full 8 weeks.

VARIATIONS

Other herbs from this book that are commonly used to make tinctures include yarrow, lavender, plantain, red clover blossoms, sage, basil, rosemary, rose, peppermint, and mugwort. They can be taken internally or used in external body care preparations, such as Yarrow Clear-Skin Topical Spray (page 145).

CAUTION: Some of these herbs may not be safe for pregnant women, people with medical issues, or women with hormone-related conditions as they act like estrogen. Please review their medicinal qualities and always do further research. You can start by reviewing the plant cautions on page 9.

Making Glycerite

A glycerin extract, known as a glycerite, is a concentrated herbal preparation made by extracting plant matter with 100 percent vegetable glycerin. I advise using an organic one. Vegetable glycerin does not extract constituents of plants as readily or as strongly as alcohol does. It is especially appropriate for drawing out the constituents of more aromatic plants, particularly their flowers and leaves. Glycerites are an ideal alternative choice for folks who do not wish to consume alcohol, and they are appropriate for children.

I make "simples," meaning one herb per formulation. If I wish to make a blend, I'll usually do that later with the finished products. Some water content is required for making a glycerite; it is unnecessary to wilt the fresh plant matter before making one.

CAUTION: Glycerites are concentrated herbal extract medicinal preparations. In other words, they are plant medicine. Before making an herbal glycerite to be taken internally, please review plant cautions on page 9 and do your research to ensure safe use.

Basic Glycerite

Makes about 2 cups (473 ml) in a pint-sized jar or 4 cups (1 L) in a quart-sized jar

Organic 100% vegetable glycerin
Fresh herbs

Fill a pint- or quart-size (473-ml or 1-L) mason jar with well-chopped, fresh herbs. I chop mine up with a pair of clean scissors as I add them to the jar. Pour glycerin over the herbs all the way to the top of the jar, making sure the plant matter is completely submerged. You can make a glycerite with dried plant matter, but since some water content is required for this preparation, you will need to add both glycerine and distilled water. Please refer to the lavender glycerite project (page 130) for instructions.

Use a clean butter knife to help release air bubbles, by gently stirring and pushing it into various parts of the mixture until you no longer see bubbles rising to the top. Label your jar with the name of the plant, whether it was fresh or dried, the solvent used for extraction, when it was bottled, and when it will be ready.

Cap it tightly and place it in a dark spot at room temperature for 6 to 8 weeks. Shake the jar occasionally. After a few days, check to see if you need to add more glycerin to fill it to the top, as plant matter will absorb some of the liquid. After 6 to 8 weeks, strain your extraction (also known as decanting) through a cheesecloth-lined strainer.

Transfer to bottles. I like using amber-tinted Boston round bottles with droppers. Affix new labels.

(continued)

Vegetable glycerin provides a sweet taste and syrupy texture but does not metabolize as sugar in the body. It is not as strong as an alcohol-based tincture; dosages are not as stringent. Adults can safely take up to 10 teaspoons (150 ml) a day, ideally spread out through the course of the day. A glycerite has a shelf life of 14 to 24 months.

VARIATIONS

Try concocting a glycerite from any of the following: lavender blossoms, rose petals, apple blossoms, mint, rosemary, dandelion blossoms and leaves, plantain leaves, mugwort blossoms and leaves, lemon balm, chamomile blossoms, violet blossoms, echinacea, nettle, mullein, skullcap, linden blossoms, or tulsi. Vegetable glycerin also does quite a good job of extracting medicines from plants with a high mucilage content, such as plantain and the roots of burdock, comfrey, and marshmallow.

Lavender Glycerite

Lavender relaxes the body, calms the mind, and uplifts the spirit. It supports the health of our respiratory and digestive systems. Lavender glycerite is easy to make all year round. Just purchase culinary-grade dried lavender in a health food store or online. You can also substitute 4 ounces (weight varies) of many other dried herbs in this recipe (see variations above).

CAUTION: Please review plant cautions on page 9 and do your research to ensure safe use.

Makes about 2 cups (473 ml) in a pint-sized jar or 4 cups (1 L) in a quart-sized jar

    4 ounces (115 g) dried lavender
    1½ cups (355 ml) 100 percent vegetable glycerin
    ½ (120 ml) cup of distilled water

Grind the lavender a bit first, using a mortar and pestle. Add the lavender to a clean pint-size (473-ml) mason jar. In a separate clean bowl, combine the glycerin and water. Pour this mixture over the herbs, filling the jar, then cap it, and allow it to sit for 6 to 8 weeks, shaking occasionally. Decant it in the same fashion as you would for fresh herbs.

Glycerites have a sweet taste and syrupy texture. Combine lavender glycerite with lemon balm glycerite and drizzle it over vanilla Greek yogurt or vanilla ice cream. Add lavender glycerite to lemonade or lemon seltzer for a delicious floral note. Lavender glycerite goes well in both iced and hot tea with a bit of lemon. Drizzle it over fruit, pancakes, or over chocolate or lemon cake. Yum! Put a little lavender glycerite in your coffee.

Making Herb-Infused Carrier Oils

Herb-infused oils, used for external body care, can be made with either fresh-wilted plant matter or dried plant matter. This is important because herbal oils are much less stable than other formulations (e.g., tinctures, glycerites, herb-infused honey, and herb-infused apple cider vinegar) and are at high risk for going rancid. Wilting for 2 to 4 days removes some of the initial moisture that can lead to spoilage in oil.

The best way to make herb-infused carrier oils is a subject of debate in the herbalism community. I've done a lot of research and experimenting, and I have learned a lot from the work of Rosemary Gladstar, Susun Weed, Deb Soule, Robin Rose Bennett, Jan Barry, April Graham, Mountain Rose Herbs, Herbal Academy, and the Chestnut School of Herbal Medicine. These are the methods I personally use for infusing oils. There are benefits and some drawbacks for each, but you'll see there is beauty in having options and getting to know your plants.

FRESH-WILTED PLANTS

"COOL" METHOD

Using fresh-wilted plant matter generally makes a superior quality oil with stronger medicinal benefits. The downside is they have some water content that when introduced into oil can lead to spoilage. Some plants—herbs such as St. John's wort, mullein flowers, violet, and arnica—only release their medicinal constituents in fresh-wilted form. I use the fresh-wilted approach as much as possible for oil quality/potency reasons, even if I wind up having to throw away some of my product. You can donate any unused oil to a biodiesel fuel company.

You must store the infusing oil in a cool, dark place with no exposure to heat for 4 to 6 weeks. Do not go beyond 6 weeks with freshly wilted plant matter, as you'll invite spoilage. I store mine in our finished basement, which never gets above 65°F (18°C). Some plants with a higher water content (like plantain) break down quickly in the oil. These should only infuse for 2 to 4 weeks with this method. Infused oils created with fresh-wilted plants will last a few months, up to 1 year, in a cool dark place. Some oils, such as olive oil and coconut oil, are more stable and will have a longer shelf life.

WILT YOUR PLANT MATTER. Do this step on a screen, in a basket, or on a large piece of cardboard, placed out of direct sunlight for 2 to 4 days. Using a dehydrator on low for a short amount of time is another option. Be sure to spread the plant matter out, cut thicker stems lengthwise and into pieces, and allow the plant matter to shrivel up some. Your aim is for it to be dry but malleable. If it dries out too much, you will lose precious nutrients.

PREPARE YOUR HERBS. Make sure your hands are clean and dry. Fill a clean, dry pint or quart-size (473-ml- to 1-L) mason jar with tight-fitting lid with roughly chopped plant matter leaving 1 inch (2.5 cm) of headspace.

ADD YOUR OIL. Pour your carrier oil of choice over the herbs, all the way to the top. You don't want any space in there for air, which can lead to oxidation. Using a clean butter knife, stir and press out the air bubbles to prevent oxidation that leads to spoilage. You'll need to add more oil, as the oil level will drop as the air bubbles rise to the top.

(continued)

Carrier Oil Choices

Olive and coconut oils are very stable. High-quality olive oil is a favorite for making salves, body butters, and some facial oils.

Jojoba oil (which is technically a liquid wax, not an oil) is also very stable. Because it is liquid wax, it will make a hard salve (more like a balm), so mix it with another carrier oil to achieve a softer texture.

Skin-friendly carrier oils include avocado, grapeseed, sunflower, safflower, hemp, apricot kernel, and almond oils.

TIPS

- Research these oils, their properties, shelf life, and whether they clog the pores.
- Experiment with oils to see which ones you like best.
- Go with either cold-pressed or expeller-pressed whenever possible.
- Always store your infused oils in a cool, dark, dry place, or refrigerate them. Using rancid oil can cause free radical damage to the body. Stored properly, your infused oils can last several months, up to 1 year (especially with the more stable oils).
- Do not use unrefined oils with fresh-wilted plant matter. It will spoil very quickly.
- Avoid using oils with a short shelf life when choosing the fresh-wilted method (such as rose hip seed oil).

LABEL YOUR JAR. Include the plant matter and oil used, date bottled, and date ready.

INFUSE. Cap and store your developing oil in a cool, dark place, generally for 4 to 6 weeks, 6 weeks maximum. For the "ready" date, I highly recommend setting a phone alert and putting it on your calendar. If it goes past 6 weeks, sadly, you must throw it away.

CHECK YOUR LEVELS. On day 2, top it off with more oil, as the plants will have absorbed some of the oil.

AVOID HEAT. Do not expose your jars to heat—this is really important to prevent spoilage. I check mine every few days for any signs of spoilage.

PAY ATTENTION. Some plants with higher water content infuse more readily into the oil and will be ready in less time (e.g., plantain in 2 to 3 weeks, and rose petals and dandelion blossoms in 4 weeks). You can see why it's important to get to know your plants.

STRAIN OUT YOUR PLANT MATTER. Use a cheesecloth-lined strainer and pour the infused oil into a new, clean jar. Do not press on the plant matter to get out any final drops with this method, as you could introduce water from the plant matter into the oil, leading to spoilage.

LET IT SIT. Allow the decanted oil to sit for several days, as any remaining water content will float to the bottom. Carefully pour your oil into a new, clean jar, leaving the water content at the bottom behind.

STORE YOUR JAR. Label your precious infused oil and place it in a cool, dry, dark place. It should be usable for several months up to 1 year, depending on the stability of the carrier oil.

DRIED PLANTS

"WARM" METHOD

Using dried plant matter will prevent spoilage—specifically the growth of bacteria, mold, and yeast—but will yield a less potent oil. Some plants with high water content are probably best infused as dry plant matter; comfrey leaf and dandelion roots are prime examples. Oils made with dried plant matter will last longer.

You can use heat for extraction and go beyond the 6-week mark. For some plant matter, such as roots, bark, and tougher plants, you will need heat to extract the most medicine.

Be sure to use a high-quality dried herb, whether you dry it yourself or purchase it.

DRY YOUR HERB. If you are working with fresh plants, fully drying a plant generally takes 2 to 4 weeks, depending on the plant and the environment you dry it in. Some dry faster, so check frequently, so as not to over-dry your plant matter, which drains it of nutrients. It should be crumbly but not so dry that it turns to dust in your grip.

GRIND YOUR FULLY DRIED HERB. Use a mortar and pestle to grind the herb.

PREPARE YOUR HERBS. Using a clean and dry jar, fill it halfway with your dried herbs. I recommend using either a pint- or quart-sized (473-ml or 1-L) mason jar, depending on the amount of infused oil you wish to make. Wide-mouth jars are easier to fill with plant matter.

ADD YOUR OIL. Pour your oil over the herbs all the way to the top. Stir and press out air bubbles with a clean butter knife. Add more oil after the air bubbles release, filling to the top line.

LABEL YOUR JAR. Cap, label, and put your oil in a warm, dry, dark place for 6 to 8 weeks. This set-up is often possible for some climates in the summer months but trickier in the winter months, unless you run a wood stove like I do, as you can put the jars near it to get the needed heat. Another alternative is to use an amber-tinted jar placed in a thick paper bag, placed in a sunny window. With this dried plant method, you will get some leakage out of the top of the jar, because oil expands when it gets warm. I put small plates and saucers under the jars to catch the oil.

STRAIN OUT YOUR PLANT MATTER. I double-strain my dried plant matter through a cheesecloth-lined strainer, as tiny bits often get caught in the oil. Use many layers of cheesecloth, or even a coffee filter. You can press the oil out of dried herbs to get every last drop.

LABEL AND STORE YOUR JAR. Transfer your oil to clean jars and label them.

Note: I do not recommend solar infusion methods because you expose your oil to direct sun. Sunlight destroys and degrades the medicinal properties of harvested herbs over time.

(continued)

SLOW COOKER METHOD

The slow cooker (Crock-Pot) method is commonly used with dried plant matter. It's not as effective as infusing dried plant matter in oil over the course of 6 to 8 weeks in a warm place, but it is a good choice if you are pinched for time. If you do choose this method, create your jar(s) of dried herbs and oil as outlined in the "warm" method, then fill your slow cooker with 2 to 3 inches of water, and place your jars of herbs and oil in the water for 8+ hours. Replenish the water as necessary, as it will evaporate. The temperature should not exceed 140°F (60°C), and the closer to 100°F (38°C) you can get, the better. Ideally, repeat this process daily, for a few days. It's not economical, as it uses a lot of electricity.

Note: For this procedure, instead of covering my jars with lids, I cover them with coffee filters secured by rubber bands. Trim the edges of the filters if they hang down too low near the water line.

The following infused oils are used in chapter 7 projects.

Dandelion Blossom–Infused Oil

Dandelion blossoms can be challenging to dry as the florets of the blooms will dry faster than the bases. I use the fresh-wilted "cool" method, allowing the blossoms to wilt for 4 days before infusing them in oil. You'll notice that the blossom heads will become white and fluffy as they dry. They are fine to use in this state, although you will have to use a lot of blossoms to fill the jar. Dandelion blossoms break down rather quickly in the oil, so you should have a potent oil in 4 weeks with this method. Use this oil to make the Dandelion and Plantain All-Purpose Healing Salve (page 138).

Plantain Leaf–Infused Oil

Plantain leaves (*Plantago major*, not the banana kind) contain a lot of water. If you choose the fresh-wilted method, roughly chop your plantain leaves and stems up right after harvesting. Wilt the chopped plant matter for 4 days before making your oil. I do not allow fresh-wilted plantain to infuse more than 2 weeks. If you go 4 to 6 weeks, your finished oil will have a short shelf life. Because plantain has a higher water content, many folks prefer to go with the dried plant "warm" method. Use this oil to make the Dandelion and Plantain All-Purpose Healing Salve (page 138).

Chocolate Mint–Infused Oil

I prefer to use fresh-wilted chocolate mint leaves from my garden, but any mint will work. Fresh mint is available year-round in grocery stores. Gently pull the leaves from the stem and fresh-wilt them for 2 to 4 days. Roughly chop them, filling your jar, following the fresh-wilted "cool" method for infusing oil. For the lip balm recipe (page 141), use coconut oil unless you have a sensitivity to it. A potent mint-infused oil will be ready in 3 to 4 weeks.

Pine Needle–Infused Oil

I live in Maine, in the middle of the woods, surrounded by pine trees that remain evergreen throughout the year. They are always available for assisting me in making infused oils that I use in formulations such as whipped body butter (page 143). I harvest only very small amounts of needles from any tree (asking the tree permission first, and abiding by the answer), and I attempt to find fresh-fallen branches after storms.

To make the infused oil, harvest enough pine needles to fill your jar. Fresh-wilt them for a few days first, then chop them up and follow the fresh-wilted "cool" method for infusing oils. I use olive oil for the body butter recipe. Your pine oil should be ready for straining in 4 to 6 weeks. If you opt to go with dried pine needles, use the dried plant "warm" method and infuse them for 6 to 8 weeks.

Making Salves

Salves are made most commonly of an herb-infused oil (or oils) and wax (usually beeswax). Good-quality olive oil is ideal for salves, both for its healing and stability properties. The beeswax provides the solid texture of the salve, besides having skin-healing constituents. For ease of use, I choose beeswax pastilles, but you can also use shavings from a block.

For basic salves, the general rule of thumb I follow is ¼ cup (40 g) of beeswax pastilles per 1 cup (240 ml) of oil.

DOUBLE BOILER METHOD

PREPARE A DOUBLE BOILER. I create my own double boiler by filling a small saucepan with 2 to 3 inches (5 to 7.5 cm) of water. I use a cleaned, recycled soup can or a small glass Pyrex measuring cup to hold the preparation.

COMBINE YOUR OILS AND BEESWAX. Put your oils and beeswax in the tin can and place it in the water bath. Be very careful not to allow any water to get into the mixture; if this happens by accident, you must discard the preparation and start again.

WARM THE PREPARATION. Heat the saucepan over low heat, stirring the preparation occasionally, until the beeswax has melted into the oil. I use a clean metal chopstick for stirring.

TEST THE CONSISTENCY. Once the beeswax has fully melted into the oil, dip a clean spoon into the liquid and place it in the freezer for about 1 minute. If you like its consistency, remove the can from your water bath and pour the hot mixture into your containers. If it feels too soft, melt a little more wax into the warm salve, and if it feels too hard, add a little bit more of your infused oil.

DRY YOUR CONTAINER. When you remove the tin can from the water bath, you must dry its base thoroughly before pouring it into your salve containers. Remember that you do not want to introduce water into the salve. I do not use essential oils in this formulation, but if you wish to, this is the time to add them.

COOL YOUR SALVE. Carefully pour the hot blend into containers and allow the salve to cool at room temperature.

LABEL AND STORE. Once fully cool, secure the lids on your containers and label them. Store your salve in a cool dark place for up to 1 year (I've actually had my olive oil salves last longer). A word of warning: Do not store your salve in a hot car; it will turn very quickly.

Dandelion and Plantain All-Purpose Healing Salve

Pairing dandelions and plantain leaves makes for a potent all-purpose healing salve and it's a must-have for your natural first-aid kit. Dandelion blossoms are highly moisturizing, heal skin, and provide pain relief. Plantain leaf heals chapped skin, reduces inflammation, disinfects and prevents infection, stops bleeding, draws toxins from insect bites, soothes sunburn, treats poison ivy, and relieves pain.

CAUTION: Please review plant cautions on page 9 and do your research to ensure safe use.

Makes approximately nine 1-ounce (28-g) salves

  ½ cup (120 ml) Dandelion Blossom–Infused Oil (page 134)
  ½ cup (120 ml) Plantain Leaf–Infused Oil (page 134)
  ¼ cup (40 g) beeswax pastilles or shavings

I infuse dandelion blossoms and plantain leaves separately in their own oil, then combine the oils to make the salve. Combine your oils and beeswax in a double boiler and follow the steps on page 136 for making a salve.

VARIATIONS

Have fun getting creative with salve-making! Why not try some of these lovely possibilities:

- A rose petal and yarrow salve for disinfecting skin, reducing inflammation, easing pain, healing wounds, and soothing sunburn and rashes

- A calming lavender salve, or a mint and rosemary salve as a chest rub or decongestant

- A mint and basil salve to ease menstrual cramps

- Experiment with lavender, garden sage, rosemary, mint, yarrow, mugwort, red clover, apple blossoms, rose petals, basil, and pine in salves, body oil, hair oil, creams, and more. Please review plant cautions on page 9.

note

Vegan options include soy wax and carnauba wax, although there are known ethical harvesting issues with carnauba wax.

Making Lip Balm

When I make a lip balm, I generally include three parts herb-infused oil, one part beeswax pastilles, and one part plant-based solid butter. Essential oils are optional, and if you plan to use them, 1 to 2 drops per tablespoon is recommended. Carrier oils that can heal, moisturize and soften your lips are olive, sweet almond, avocado, coconut, and sunflower. Jojoba is a liquid wax and will make a harder balm. Castor oil will add a little bit of gloss to your finished product. Healing, nourishing butters include shea, mango, and cocoa.

DOUBLE BOILER METHOD

PREPARE A DOUBLE BOILER. I create my own by filling a small saucepan with 2 to 3 inches (5 to 7.5 cm) of water. I prefer to use a small glass Pyrex measuring cup to hold the preparation, as the spout makes for more controlled pouring into tubes and smaller tins. However, if you're putting the lip balm into a larger tin, you can also use a cleaned, recycled soup can instead of the Pyrex measuring cup.

COMBINE YOUR INGREDIENTS. Place all your ingredients except the essential oil in the tin can and place it in the water bath. Be very careful not to allow any water to get into the mixture. If this happens by accident, you must discard the preparation and start again.

WARM THE PREPARATION. Heat the saucepan over low heat, stirring the mixture occasionally, until the beeswax and butter have melted into the oil. I use a clean metal chopstick for stirring.

TEST THE CONSISTENCY. Once the beeswax and butter have fully melted into the oil, dip a clean spoon into the liquid and place it in the freezer for about 1 minute. If you like its consistency, remove the measuring cup from your water bath and pour the hot mixture into your containers. If it feels too soft, melt a little more wax into the warm balm, and if it feels too hard, add a little bit more infused oil.

DRY YOUR CONTAINER. When you remove the measuring cup from the water bath, you must dry its base thoroughly before pouring it into your containers. Remember that you do not want to introduce water into the balm. If you wish to add essential oils to this formulation, now is the time to add them.

POUR YOUR BALM. There's a trick to pouring the balm into the tubes so you get a solid and smooth finish. If you pour the oil in at once, you'll get a sinker hole in the middle. To get a nice smooth finish, pour a tiny bit into the tube and allow it to get semi-solid, then pour more and wait again, repeating this process until you fill the tube. Be careful when pouring, as it's very hot. Fully cool at room temperature.

LABEL AND STORE. Once fully cool, secure the lids on your containers and label them. Store your lip balm in a cool dark place for up to 1 year.

Vanilla Chocolate Mint Lip Balm

I enjoy making herb-infused lip balms, especially with peppermint, chocolate mint, and orange mint. You can also use peppermint or spearmint for this recipe. The cocoa butter adds its own rich chocolatey layer to the finished balm. Along with a pleasurable sensory experience, mint provides anti-inflammatory properties that soothe, cool, and heal the lips.

I use fractionated coconut oil here, because I like the texture and it does not have an overpowering smell. Some people are sensitive to coconut oil and find it to be drying to their skin, so those folks should pick another oil.

CAUTION: Please review plant cautions on page 9 and do your research to ensure safe use.

Makes approximately six ¼-ounce (7-g) tubes or approximately three ½-ounce (14-g) tins of lip balm

> 3 tablespoons (45 ml) Chocolate Mint–Infused Oil (page 135)
> 1 tablespoon (1 g) beeswax pastilles or shavings
> 1 tablespoon (15 g) cocoa butter shavings
> 5 to 10 drops vanilla oleoresin essential oil (optional)

Combine the infused oil, beeswax, and cocoa butter in a double boiler. Follow the instructions for making a lip balm (page 139), adding the optional essential oil just before pouring the oil.

VARIATIONS

Consider making lip balms with carrier oils infused with rose petals, plantain, apple blossoms, and dandelion blossoms.

note

Vegan options include soy wax and carnauba wax, although there are known ethical harvesting issues with carnauba wax.

note

I also infuse the leaves of the Eastern red cedar tree into the same oil (pictured here), as it has pain-relieving constituents. Infuse both into olive oil.

Woodland Whipped Body Butter

There is nothing better than meandering through a forest, inhaling the fresh, invigorating scent of evergreen trees. That's the experience I've captured in this nourishing, decadent whipped body butter, layered with scents of pine, cedarwood, woodsy juniper, and sweet vanilla. Pine can lift your mood, increase circulation, and ease muscle and nerve pain.

The formulation consists of two main ingredients—carrier oil (or oils) and a plant-based butter, whipped to a fluffy consistency. Butters, such as shea, mango, and cocoa, are ultra-hydrating and especially beneficial to skin in the winter months.

CAUTION: Please review plant cautions on page 9 and do your research to ensure safe use.

Makes approximately three 4-ounce (120-ml) mason jars

¼ cup (60 ml) Pine Needle–Infused Oil (page 135)
¼ cup (60 ml) sweet almond oil or another carrier oil
½ cup (118 g) shea, cocoa, or mango butter

3 drops vanilla essential oil
4 drops cedarwood essential oil (avoid if pregnant)
7 drops juniper essential oil (avoid if pregnant)

Place all the ingredients except the essential oils in a double boiler. Warm over low heat until the butter fully melts into the oil.

Transfer to your stand mixer's stainless-steel bowl or a mixing bowl of your choice if using a hand mixer.

Place in the refrigerator for approximately 1½ hours, or until the temperature cools to 55°F to 60°F (13°C to 16°C). I use a clean digital meat thermometer to check the temperature.

Whip the preparation on high with your mixer for approximately 5 minutes, until the mixture turns to a white, fluffy cream with stiff peaks. Add essential oils during the whipping process.

Transfer to clean, airtight containers.

VARIATION

Many plants in this book can be infused into oils and whipped into a body butter. Consider lavender, garden sage, rosemary, mint, plantain, dandelion blossoms, rose petals, and red clover. Please review plant cautions on page 9.

notes

- If you prefer not to use essential oils, that is fine. The pine-infused oil will impart a fresh scent combined with the aroma of shea butter, which is smoky and mildly fruity (depending on the brand and batch you get, as I have received some with a strong nutty scent).

- You may wish to make whipped body butters during the cooler months, as warmer temperatures can take away the whipped quality you worked so hard to achieve. If you do make it in the warmer months as I do, or if you're in a warmer climate, refrigerate the finished product or keep it in an air-conditioned space.

Yarrow Clear-Skin Topical Spray

The essential ingredient of this medicinal topical spray is the common yarrow plant—the white-flowered original plant. It grows wild in abundance where I live here in Maine, and probably in your region too, but if you can't harvest it yourself, you can buy dried yarrow. Yarrow gifts us with antibacterial, anti-inflammatory, astringent, and exfoliating properties. It naturally contains salicylic acid, a key ingredient in most anti-acne treatment that can deeply penetrate skin, loosen, and dissolve dead skin cells and dirt that clogs pores. This topical spray can help heal existing acne on the face and body and prevent future breakouts, keeping skin soft, smooth, and firm.

CAUTION: Please review plant cautions on page 9 and do your research to ensure safe use.

Makes 13 ounces (384 ml)

3 ounces (88 ml) yarrow tincture (follow the directions on page 125)

10 ounces (296 ml) distilled water

Combine the tincture with the distilled water.

Label your finished spray and store it in a cool dark place, or refrigerate it for up to 6 months. Shake the bottle before each use.

Spritz on clean, damp skin once a day—twice if your skin is not prone to dryness. Spray it onto acne-prone areas on the face and body (avoiding the eyes), or apply it in a targeted way with a Q-tip. It also works wonderfully as a bug repellent.

Rosemary and Lavender Dry Spray Shampoo

Rosemary and lavender are beneficial to the scalp, specifically boosting circulation that in turn promotes strong hair and hair growth. That's why I like to work with them to make hair growth oil and dry spray shampoo. Rosemary has darkening properties, so if you have light locks, just stick with the lavender in this recipe. If you're a fan of dry shampoo, but not a fan of chemicals, I think you'll fancy this homemade natural option.

CAUTION: Please review plant cautions on page 9 and do your research to ensure safe use.

Makes just over ¼ cup (75 ml)

1 tablespoon (15 ml) Lavender and Rosemary–Infused Witch Hazel (see below)

¼ cup (60 ml) distilled water
1 tablespoon (9 g) arrowroot powder or cornstarch
2 drops of your favorite essential oil (optional)

Combine all the ingredients in a clean bowl or container, mixing them well. Transfer to a 4-ounce (120-ml) spray bottle. Shake well before each use. Spray on roots and oily parts of your hair. Allow to dry in the hair. You can comb it through if you'd like.

Lavender and Rosemary-Infused Witch Hazel

Fill a clean jar halfway with ground, fully dried rosemary and lavender, or halfway with lavender if you have light hair, then pour witch hazel over the herbs all the way to the top of the jar. Cap it and allow it to steep for 2 weeks. Check it after a few days, and add more witch hazel if necessary, as the plant matter will absorb it. Strain out the plant matter and place your infused witch hazel in a clean jar. The dry shampoo requires only 1 tablespoon (15 ml) of witch hazel, so any extra can be used as a facial toner or saved to make future shampoo. Lavender and rosemary both promote clear skin and heal acne.

CHAPTER 8

Working with Herbs in Spellwork, Rituals, and Divination Practice

"Magic is the use of the natural forces of nature
to bring about needed changes."

—Scott Cunningham, *Earth Power*

Plants are a natural force. They contain energies—each holding a spiritual vibration that is individual and unique. Working in partnership with these green energies can give a power boost to your spellwork, rituals, and divination and amplify the intentions behind them. This begins with getting to know each plant intimately and understanding their magickal correspondences. That's plant magick.

In these projects, you'll experience the thirteen essential plants in a hands-on way, incorporating herbs into magickal practices to amplify their power and effectiveness. Follow my suggestions for these projects, use them as a springboard for other ideas, or go in your own direction. Always honor your personal relationships with certain plants, in addition to the traditional correspondences. Remember, our personal relationship with each plant is what matters most, even if it differs from established magickal correspondences.

Spellwork and the Meaning of Magick

I've thought a lot about the meaning of *magick* and what it is exactly, and here is what my heart speaks. Witches practice magick through spellwork and divination practice. They get in touch with their own personal power. They work in concert with nature and the Universe to raise, harness, and direct energies to produce positive change. That's really all there is to it. It's a natural and down-to-earth process.

A spell is a form of magick that involves setting a specific intention around a particular situation to bring about transformation. Magickal intentions are simply human needs and wants. Common themes include love, protection, healing, happiness, luck, money, wishes, and cleansing negative energies. Spellwork refers to all that goes into crafting and carrying out your spells, sending them out into the Universe through a series of steps. It's also known as spellcasting or simply "casting."

A spell can be an elaborate ritual, or it can be performed in a much more practical way. I am of the belief that spells do not require highly formalized steps: A simple act fueled by intention is no less powerful than a full-on ritual. Some of the most powerful spells are the ones you craft for yourself, with the personal power you hold within, because no one else knows you or your situation better than you do.

As a green witch, I prefer a casting process that incorporates the use of herbs. For example, I may craft a spell jar for protection and enhanced psychic awareness. The very act of creating the spell jar is a spell in itself, whether or not you choose to do a more formal spell with the jar. Intuit and choose what feels right and doable to you in any given situation. Explore different practices and see what feels comfortable to you.

Creating Spells

Whether you are drawing on a spell for inspiration or creating your own from scratch, it helps to plan steps ahead of time, especially if you are new to casting. Here are steps you can follow to prepare a formal spellcasting ritual:

SET A CLEAR INTENTION. Your spell centers around your need or want. It could be for yourself, another individual, or for a community. For the best result, it's important to have a specific focus and aim.

TAKE TIME TO CONSIDER THE CONSEQUENCES. Drawing on your intuition, think about what you want to occur, and carefully consider and imagine all possible outcomes. The spell should be ethical (for example, I'm not comfortable with spells that involve manipulation and coercion).

CREATE THE SPELL. With your clear intention in mind, put your spell into words. It can be written down or conjured in your mind. It may rhyme and have poetic flair, but that's not necessary.

GATHER INGREDIENTS AND TOOLS. Magickal tools act as ancient, powerful symbols that can support you in your spellwork by helping you get in touch with your own energy and the natural energy around you and by amplifying your intentions. Incorporate correspondences such as herbs or crystals that correlate with the spell you are casting. Possibilities for supplies include a cauldron, besom (witch's broom), wand, athame (ritual knife), cup, pentagram, incense, candle, candle snuffer, chalice, music, or bell.

DECIDE WHEN AND WHERE YOU WILL PERFORM YOUR SPELL. Consider activating your spell during a particular moon phase, month, or day of the week with energies that match and support your desired outcome. For example, the waxing moon phase is an ideal time for casting spells around abundance, success, and friendship. Fridays are also associated with friendship, so you could doubly amplify a friendship spell by casting it on a Friday during a waxing moon. However, for timing, sometimes urgency must be observed regardless of correspondences.

The Power of Elemental Magick

Drawing on the elements can help you to raise the energy required for your spell by allowing you to tap into and connect with the natural vibrations of the Universe, which you'll work in concert with to carry out your spellwork. If the energy comes solely from you, you'll quickly become depleted, so allow the greater energy to flow through you. Draw the needed energy up from the Earth through the roots of your "tree," and release it when you are ready to send your intention out into the Universe. Grounding yourself and raising energy can also take place before the spellcasting ritual, in the form of a purifying ritual bath (page 173), a walk through the forest, working in the garden, or having an orgasm (sex magick is powerful).

Spellcasting

When you are ready to cast your spell, begin by clearing your mind and removing any distractions. Cleanse the energies of your casting space and your aura with a "sweep" of your besom or a sprinkle of salt. Cast a circle of protection around your space through visualization, gesture, and/or spoken word. I prefer to physically cast my circle either with my wand or with smoke from a burning herb bundle (page 170). A circle of salt that encompasses your area can also be created (page 175).

GROUND YOURSELF THROUGH VISU-ALIZATION AND GESTURE. Witches often envision themselves as a tree, with strong roots for grounding and upper parts that reach out into the ether.

SET THE TONE. Enter into a meditative or even trance-like state through more visualization, music, drumming, dance, the tone of a bell, burning incense, or holding a crystal. You may wish to dress a candle with selected herbs that correspond with your intention (page 163). You can also decorate the base of the candle with corresponding crystals. Light the candle and vocalize your intention, sending it out into the Universe, releasing the energy.

FOCUS ON YOUR INTENTION. You can speak, sing, or chant your intention out loud. Think it in your mind or use gestures; it's up to you.

CAST YOUR SPELL. When I cast, I state my intention positively and firmly, as if the outcome already exists. I seal the spell by asking it to be carried out "correctly" with harm to none. If you're burning an intentional candle, allow it to burn out on its own. Snuff it out if you must, but do not blow it out.

REGROUND YOURSELF. After you cast your spell, take time to focus on your breath and be fully aware of your surroundings. Crack a window and feel the breeze on your cheek. Grabbing a snack can also do the trick. I take time to tidy up my sacred space, put away my tools, and whisk my besom across the space to clear and neutralize the energy.

Evaluate how the spell plays out over time. After you send the spell out into the Universe, give it a little distance and time to do its thing, but also take notes on its efficacy. It may be what you expect, or it may not. The Universe, which includes the energy of your Higher Self, may have other plans than what your conscious mind envisions. Once the outcome presents itself, show gratitude. Often your spell will require you to do some further work to make it happen, as opposed to sitting back and waiting. After all, it is spell *work*.

The more experienced you become with spellcasting, the more quickly you'll be able to go through the key components of these steps, with little planning, in any given moment, with or without magickal tools, when your help is needed. In fact, it happened to me at the grocery store the other day after having a conversation with a person who was elderly, wheelchair-bound, alone, and having a difficult time. After we spoke and I continued to shop, I crafted a spell on the spot in my mind to send this person love, protection, and warmth. No onlooker would have ever known I was casting. I didn't have tools or my sacred ritual space, but the intention in my heart and the energy I called forth were strong, and that's all that was needed.

The Thirteen Herbs in Spellwork, Rituals, and Divination Practice

There is something so special and enchanting about using herbs in your magickal practice that you have either reverently foraged or grown in your garden. These experiences put you in direct contact with the living, growing plants in your environment and allow you to forge a spiritual connection with them—one that carries over into working with them, making it that much more meaningful and powerful. Let's get to the making!

CAUTION: If a plant in this book is new to you, consume only a small amount at first if it is edible, to see how your body reacts, and do a patch test for a topical preparation before full application. For instance, some people have allergies to plants in the Asteraceae family, which includes chamomile, daisy, and ragweed (dandelion, mugwort, and yarrow in this book are in this plant family). Be sure to read the disclaimer in full and review plant cautions (page 9) before experimenting with the projects in this chapter. It's also important to do your own research.

Divination

Divination comes from the Latin *divinare* which means "to forsee." It is an art form used to connect with the Divine as a means of tapping into collective knowledge and wisdom that comes from the Higher Self, the Collective Unconscious, and the Spirit World (through guides, ancestors, goddesses/gods). These sources are interconnected and a part of the Divine Tapestry of Life.

Divination practices include:

- tarot reading
- runes
- palmistry
- tea leaf readings (tasseomancy)
- pendulum work
- scrying—gazing at a crystal ball (crystallomancy), water (hydromancy), or smoke.

Divination provides answers to our questions about future outcomes, yes, but it does so much more beyond fortune-telling. It allows us to be more in tune—with ourselves, with others, and beyond. It encourages spiritual growth, empowers us, and provides healing and inspiration that can fuel our ambitions. We glean information that can be used in service to the greater good.

With practice, divination allows us to become sensitive to energies all around us and hones our sixth sense, which I believe we all have in varying strengths. Divination practice can put us in touch with our wants and needs and the wants and needs of others. It can inform and guide our spellwork that we perform to bring about positive, needed change. It invites open-mindedness, encourages us to think creatively, and stimulates ideas and creativity. Divination practice allows us to self-reflect and evolve in a more mindful way.

Scrying

Scrying is a form of divination used to obtain helpful knowledge and guidance.

Scrying is also used to see into the future and for making predictions. I support scrying because using it as a tool for the present moment feels most beneficial. It can ground you, give clarity and direction, and provide you with a warm, supportive energy that fortune-telling can lack.

There are a variety of ways to scry. You can gaze into a reflective surface such as a mirror, flame, crystal ball (known as crystallomancy), or a dark bowl filled with water (hydromancy). You can even use something more unconventional, such as dappled light on a surface or a puddle of water on the ground. I believe that the key to a positive, successful scrying session has less to do with the tools and more to do with state of mind when engaging in the practice.

Achieving a relaxed state before scrying is a must. To help you get there, you can try the following:

- Apply divination anointing oil (page 155) or a witch's "flying" ointment to pulse points (page 178).

- Burn your favorite herbal incense (page 167).

- Sip a relaxing intentional tea for psychic clarity (page 161).

- Light a candle and burn an herb bundle (page 170).

- Listen to singing bowls music or play your own singing bowl.

- Wrap a cozy blanket around your body.

Allow your whole body to relax. Allow your thoughts to soften and recede as you gaze into the reflective surface. Your eyelids may begin to lightly flutter.

The messages and insights you receive will come through your preferred clairvoyance modality. Perhaps it's visual or audial, or a combination of modalities. You may receive messages from loved ones who have passed over, or perhaps receive a general, more collective perception, like thoughts that come from the Higher Self or Collective Unconscious.

Divination Anointing Oil

I created this herbal oil to aid me in spirit communication, but it can assist you with any magickal practice that involves psychic ability. It's filled with herbs, spices, and essential oils to help you tap into and enhance those extrasensory abilities. Use this charged oil to anoint candles, crystals, tools, and yourself before practicing divination with tarot, scrying (page 154), runes, tea leaf reading, and more.

CAUTION: Please review plant cautions on page 9 and do your research to ensure safe use.

Dried rose petals for protection and psychic intuition
A few poppyseeds for encouraging visions
Mugwort-infused carrier oil (page 131)
   to support clairvoyance and the summoning of spirits
3 drops of essential oils (optional; see note)
Pinch of cinnamon to improve psychic ability by increasing vibration
Small amethyst crystal or selenite crystal for protection and sharpening
   clairvoyance

Place the dried rose petals in the jar. Pour in the poppyseeds, using a funnel if you prefer. Pour the oil over them and add the essential oils (if using). Add the pinch of cinnamon and your crystal. You need not strain out the dried plant matter or crystal.

To use the oil, pour a couple of drops into your hands and rub them together, warming up the oil. It feels comforting and smells wonderful and witchy. Apply it to your skin, especially to your pulse points, your Heart Center, and Third Eye region. Use the remaining light film of oil on your hands to anoint your magickal tools. You may even elect to take a ritual bath graced with a few drops of this anointing oil before engaging in a divination or spirit communication session.

note

I add 1 drop of vanilla oleoresin oil to raise my vibrational energy and 2 drops of vetiver, which promotes psychic awareness and hones intuition. Vetiver is also known to help you connect with fae spirit energies, and it is one of my favorite scents. This blend smells deeply woodsy with the added hint of vanilla—yes, it's heavenly.

CAUTION: Avoid vetiver if pregnant.

Love Spell Anointing Oil

This anointing oil calls your soulmate to you, but you can get creative and alter the spell to make it work for any type of love.

On the night of the New Moon, put eight fresh-wilted or dried rose petals into a small, pretty bottle. Cover them with fractionated coconut oil or another skin-friendly oil. Gently shake the bottle each day, envisioning the qualities you desire in your mate.

On the eve of the Full Moon, strain out the petals. Use the oil to anoint your Heart Center, to open it and draw your soulmate to you.

On this eve of the full silver moon,
my heart's desires are clear.
I anoint myself with oil of rose
to draw my soulmate ever near.
With harm to none, this spell has begun.

Love Spell Ethics

Love spells. They are a bit of a controversial topic in the witch community, especially when it comes to romantic love. Do I cast them? Yes, but never so it attempts to manipulate or control someone against their will.

There are plenty of ways to cast love spells of good intention—and ones that work with feelings and thoughts that already exist. You can send love to someone (or a group of people) in need of it. Love spells can also work to mend a relationship or draw more love into your life. They can also be used to increase your charisma or enhance and strengthen an existing relationship. And love spells need not be limited to the earthly realm. I frequently use them to send love to spirits on the other side.

Spell Jars

Spell jars were used in the sixteenth and seventeenth centuries in England and North America, as amulets to protect against malevolent magick and evil spirits. Originally known as witch bottles, they were concocted to protect new homes and to return a harmful spell back to the "witch" who supposedly cast it. Early witch bottles were made of salt-glazed stoneware and filled with strange ingredients such as the "victim's" urine, hair, and fingernails, small animal bones, pins often pushed into felt or cloth hearts, and nails, then either buried in the earth for protection or thrown into a fire or tossed into a river or stream to be rid of the supposed "witch."

Today, modern witches create their own versions of these jars, which are used for a wider variety of intentions—not exclusively for protection from negative energies. Spell jars often contain sand, coins, wood, shells, feathers, knotted threads, stones and crystals, red wine, sea water, salt, vinegar, oil, ashes, or, of course, herbs. Make your own witch's spell jar by filling a small glass bottle with herbs and crystals that have magickal properties associated with your intent. Change these up based on your needs and availability of herbs.

VARIATIONS

Here are some other dried herbal and crystal combinations you may wish to try.

LOVE: rose petals, apple seeds, and yarrow, with rose quartz

HEALING: pine needles, plantain, mint, with clear quartz

HAPPINESS AND HARMONY: basil, sage, rose petals, with a desert rose stone

PROSPERITY AND ABUNDANCE: mint, dandelion, clover, and jade or citrine

For Relaxing Sleep Laced with Vivid, Prophetic Dreams

Fill your bottle with dried mugwort, lavender, and amethyst crystal. All three work together to provide protection and promote a calm sleep, vivid dreams, and psychic visions. Seal the jar with candle wax, and as long as the seal stays intact, the potency of its magick will remain.

You can also anoint the jar with an intentional oil that matches the theme of your bottle. Refer to the anointing oil recipe for instructions, substituting your herbs of choice (page 155), and recite your wishes. Maybe something like . . .

Mugwort, lavender, amethyst divine,
dance within this spell jar of mine.
Protect and grant me peace in the night.
Bestow upon me your gifts of blessed sight.

Place the bottle on your altar or in a place where you would like its influence to work. I place this one on my bedside table.

Intentional Tea Blends

The ancient ritual of brewing and enjoying a hot cup of herbal tea soothes the body, heart, and mind. It invites you to slow down, take pause, and be present in the moment as you enjoy its flavor, aroma, and radiating warmth. I love to craft herbal tea blends with plants that I've foraged, grown in my garden, harvested, and processed with my own hands . . . plants rooted in the earth, touched by the rays of the sun and moon, bathed in rain, and kissed by the wind. This magick is contained in a single cup of tea.

You can wildcraft intentional teas with plants that will gift you with both medicinal and magickal benefits. If these herbs are new to you, try them one at a time as a tea, ingesting only a bit to make sure the herb agrees with you.

I use 1 heaping teaspoon of dried tea blend per boiling cup of water, allowing it to steep 10 to 15 minutes. To better release the herbs's properties, crush them first, using a mortar and pestle. To sweeten, I use a dollop of homemade herb-infused honey (page 123).

CAUTION: Mugwort makes a strong tea that should be used mindfully. To be safe, I recommend refraining from driving or operating machinery after drinking this tea. Please review plant cautions on page 9 and do your research to ensure safe use.

VARIATIONS

LOVE TEA BLENDS

- Rose petals, chocolate mint, tulsi (holy basil), chamomile, dashes of cardamom and chocolate (associated with lust and love), sweetened with rose petal–infused honey (page 123)
- Rose petals and apple blossoms with rose petal-infused honey

PSYCHIC ENHANCEMENT TEA BLENDS

- Mugwort, mint, dandelion leaves. Dandelion leaf and mugwort taste bitter (pleasantly so in my opinion), so add some honey.
- Yarrow with honey and lemon to give it a milder taste
- Rosemary (fresh, if available) and lavender with lemon and honey
- Mugwort, rose petals, mint, and lavender

PEACE AND CALM

- Lavender, lemon balm, chamomile, and marshmallow root

VITALITY

- Pine needles with fresh lemon and honey

(continued)

PROTECTION AND PURIFICATION

- Sage and mint (I like to crush fresh wild black-berries and add their delicious juice to this tea.)

HAPPINESS AND HARMONY

- Peppermint and basil with a pinch of carda-mom and cloves

BLESSINGS AND GOOD FORTUNE

- Tulsi, rose petals, and fresh ginger

FOCUS AND CLARITY

- Rosemary, red clover, mint, lemon, and honey

SLEEP AND VIVID DREAMS

- Lavender, mugwort, rose petals, and passionflower

TASSEOMANCY

Tasseomancy is a form of divination by way of reading tea leaves. Simply grind your tea blend herbs very finely in your mortar and pestle and place them in a white or cream-colored mug for easy viewing, preferably a larger, round one. Or you can use a special tasseomancy teacup. Pour hot water over your herbs, allowing them to brew as you normally would.

Drink your tea after the herbs have settled to the bottom of the cup, leaving a little liquid behind. Envision a question in your mind as you sip the tea, preferably a question that corresponds to the intention of your magickal tea blend. Swirl the remaining liquid and herbs in your cup, counterclockwise, three times.

Magick with Intentional Teas

- Stir your tea clockwise to enhance its intention.
- Amplify your spellwork with an intentional tea that matches the theme. Sip the tea as you cast the spell.
- Charge your magickal tools with the tea: Wipe them with a soft cloth dipped in the liquid.
- Sprinkle or spritz some of the tea in the area where you will be casting your spell.
- Add some intentional tea to a warm ritual bath. Put some in a drawstring muslin bag or sachet that you steep in the bathwater. Bathe in it while sipping a cup of the same tea, amplifying its power.
- Spritz some intentional tea into a soft cloth and use it to dust the sacred space of your home. This works well with blends that promote love or happiness and harmony or that protect and cleanse negative energies.

Place the cup upside down on the saucer and leave it be for three minutes. Pick up the cup and view the patterns inside of it. This is your reading. Intuit what you see in the tea leaves. What do the symbols mean to you, personally?

If you are interested in learning more about tasseomancy, there are plenty of resources available on the subject. As with dream interpretation, there are commonly accepted meanings for symbols, although I think making your own personal interpretations based on the context of your own life experience is a powerful, effective way to interpret what you see in your teacup.

Candle Dressing

Candles are the perfect embodiment of Elemental magick because when you burn a candle you involve all the elements: Fire in the flame. Earth in the wax (either beeswax or a plant-based wax). Air in the oxygen that feeds the flame. Water as the wax melts into liquid form. And ether or Spirit contained in all things and binds together all the elements.

A candle can be charged with your magickal intention and covered in herbs that correspond with that intention, called dressing a candle. When you burn it, the elements work together to send your intention, boosted by the powers of the herbs, out into the Universe to manifest. That makes for some potent magick, don't you think?

I dress my tapered candles in one of two ways.

METHOD 1: Anoint your candle with vegetable-based oil and then cover it with herbs that correspond with your intention. For example, crushed mint leaves make the perfect candle dressing for intentions around prosperity and abundance.

Sigils

You may choose to carve a sigil into the wax. A sigil is a personal symbol that represents an intention or desired outcome. Design one on paper first by writing a word that encapsulates your intention. Delete any repeating letters. Here's the fun part: Use the remaining letters to create a graphic symbol. Use upper- or lower-case letters, print, script, or a combination of these things. Position and combine the letters as you wish, having them touch, to create a singular symbol. Keep going until you achieve a design that speaks to you. The result is your own unique and powerful sigil.

Make sure that the oil you choose can withstand the heat: Olive and avocado oils are good choices. Generally, if it's safe for cooking with, you can use it to dress your candle.

Grind your herb or herbs of choice very finely in a mortar and pestle, then place them on a piece of waxed paper. Warm a little oil in your hands, then roll the candle back and forth in your hands, coating it with oil. Place the oiled candle in the herbs, coating it with the herbs. Put the dressed candle in a candle holder.

METHOD 2: Grind your herbs in a mortar and pestle and set them aside. Using a hair dryer, heat up a portion of a clean-burning beeswax or soy-based candle. Press herbs into the softened wax. Continue this process all over the candle, covering it in herbs.

CAUTION: Remember that some herbs emit toxins when burned. Herbs from this book that are safe to burn include rose, lavender, mugwort, garden sage, mint, dandelion, rosemary, basil, pine needles, and apple blossoms. Never leave a candle unattended, and keep a close eye on candles dressed with oil and herbs.

Burn your dressed candle in a safe spot. I put mine on my altar. I sometimes cast an accompanying spell—although not always, as the act of dressing and burning the candle with intention serves as a spell. Then I allow it to work its magick, sending my intention out into the ether. Allow it to burn out all the way. Or, if you must extinguish it due to time constraints, lore suggests it's better to snuff out the flame than blow it out.

(continued)

WAYS TO USE DRESSED CANDLES

- Dress candles with mugwort, rose petals, and lavender to give a boost to your psychic abilities. I place these on the small circular table where I do my work with divination and spirit communication.

- Dress and burn candles for various rituals and celebrations. For Yule, I dress candles with dried, crushed mint and pine needles for joy, health, abundance, and prosperity and incorporate them into our family's Yule log with balsam fir clippings.

- Offer herb-dressed candles to a spirit guide, ancestor, or deity. Artemis is often associated with healing herbs, so I like to dress a candle in dried herbs that correspond to healing (such as lavender, mint, plantain, mugwort clover, pine, and apple blossoms) and burn the dressed candle in her name. If you wish to invoke a spiritual entity to help you in either your spellwork or in your practice of divination, it's a wonderful way to show thanks for their guidance and assistance.

- Burn your intentional candle on a particular day of the week with an energy that matches your intent. Sundays are good for healing and prosperity. Monday for travel and animals. Tuesday for strength. Wednesday for business deals, divination, and knowledge. Thursday for legal matters and job-related issues. Friday for love. Saturday for communication and meditation.

Color Magick

Choose a candle color that corresponds with your intention.

- **White for spirit**
- **Black for cleansing negative energies**
- **Green for abundance and prosperity**
- **Orange for success with legal issues**
- **Pink for love**
- **Red for strength, protection, and passion**
- **Yellow for clarity**
- **Purple for healing**
- **Dark blue for psychic powers**
- **Light blue for calm**
- **Brown for grounding**
- **Gray for neutrality**
- **Gold for money**
- **Silver for peace**

- Align the dressing and burning of your candle with a particular moon phase. The new moon is perfect for beginning new endeavors, which are then grown in congruence with the increasing energy of the waxing moon. Each full moon has characteristics that can teach us valuable lessons. The waning moon is ideal for slowing down, relaxing, reflecting, and tying up any loose ends.

You can magnify the power of your intentional magick by combining some of these correspondences. For instance, you might dress a dark blue candle with mugwort and burn it on a Wednesday to amplify your psychic ability, as all three are associated with this theme. Keep in mind that your intention is always the most important and powerful factor. Herbs, color magick, and timing correspondences can give power boosts to the energy you are releasing.

Herbal and Resin Incense

I like to burn incense for different purposes—for pleasure; to serve as a mystical backdrop for my rituals, divination practices, and spellwork; and for its specific magickal properties and vibrations that can support the intents of my magickal workings. For example, I burn a pinch of the Protection and Purification incense blend while casting a circle of protection before scrying. I'll then burn the Psychic Powers and Divination incense (page 168) to amplify my psychic powers needed for successful scrying (page 154).

I particularly love burning herbs that I've foraged or grown in my garden, as this deepens and empowers the experience. Many of the sweet-smelling plants don't give off an aromatic scent when burned, but that's not usually of concern to me when it comes to burning them for spellwork, as I'm more focused on working with their energies than their scents.

Sometimes I wildcraft herb bundles (page 170), or I may burn individual dried leaves or petals in a fireproof dish. My favorite method is to grind the dried plant matter in my mortar and pestle and burn it on an incense charcoal tablet in a heat-proof vessel (left).

Plants, Spices, and Resins for Burning

HERBS (DRIED): rose petals, apple (seeds, blossoms, and bark), lavender, mugwort, garden sage, mint, dandelion, yarrow, rosemary, basil, pine needles, blue spruce needles, Eastern red cedar needles, juniper, bay leaf, mullein, sweetfern, lemongrass, calendula, lilac, lemon balm, chamomile, marshmallow root, catnip, dill, thyme, amaranth, eucalyptus.

SPICES, FRUITS (DRIED): cinnamon, cloves, juniper berries, allspice, ginger, citrus fruit rinds.

RESINS: frankincense, copal, dragons blood, benzoin, myrrh.

Sometimes I incorporate a resin into the plant-based incense, especially if its magickal properties align with my work, and because resins will produce a pleasant aroma and allow the incense to smolder longer. I simply grind up the resin tears in my mortar and pestle, using a pounding motion. It can get a little sticky, so I process it separately from the plant matter. Some people use a drop or two of essential oil to sweeten the smell of their herbal incense, but I don't recommend using both a resin and essential oil, as they both produce some moisture (which can prevent your incense from burning).

(continued)

Place your charcoal tablet inside a heatproof container. The tablet is shaped like a bowl, so put it in the vessel, open side up. For added safety, line the container with salt or sand. Ignite the edges of the disc while it sits in the container, and once it catches fire, sprinkle a little dried, ground-up herbs and powdered resin into its center. It should smoke immediately.

CAUTION: A charcoal tablet is made specifically for burning incense in; it's not the same as charcoal used for the grill. Be sure to burn herbs and incense safely: Do this in a well-ventilated area, by a cracked window or out in the open air. The vessel will get very hot, so be careful not to burn yourself, and do not place it near or on a flammable surface. It's important to always do your research, as some plants put off toxins when burned. If you have asthma or other breathing issues, or if you are pregnant, I do not recommend the use of herbal smoke.

HERBS TO BE USED AS INCENSE	
THEME/CORRESPONDENCE	HERBS
Love	lavender, basil, rose petals, yarrow, pine needles, apple (seeds, blossoms, and bark)
Protection and Purification	basil, garden sage, mugwort, rosemary, rose petals, yarrow, pine needles
Healing	lavender, mint, garden sage, mugwort, rose petals, apple (seeds, blossoms, and bark)
Prosperity and Abundance	mint, dandelion, apple (seeds, blossoms, and bark)
Psychic Powers and Divination	mint, dandelion, mugwort, garden sage, rose petals, yarrow, apple (seeds, blossoms, and bark)

Smoke Cleansing

The burning of herbs as incense is a sacred practice of many traditions. Pinches of dried herbs can be burned in heatproof censers in special charcoal discs meant specifically for burning incense, or they can be burned as dried bundles. I may have missed my calling as a florist, as I enjoy making smoke-cleansing herbal bundles that are actually more like herbal bouquets artfully designed and created with the plants' magickal properties in mind.

Herb bundles are burned for a variety of reasons. They can be burned to clear stagnant or negative energy in a room to make room for beneficial energy, to reduce stress and anxiety, to mark a significant event, to help you center, ground, and relax in preparation for spiritual work, or for celebratory purposes such as observing a sabbat. You can create an intentional bundle that matches the theme of your spellwork and, as you burn the bouquet, your intentions will be sent out upon its smoke, amplified by the magickal properties of the plants.

Remember that it's not necessary to burn these bundles to tap into their energy. Witches with asthma or other respiratory conditions often refrain from this practice. Instead, you can use the bouquets in your rituals just like you would a wand or a besom.

When it comes to designing smoke-cleansing herbal bouquets, let your creativity run wild. Certain plants will look gorgeous together, but you'll also want to keep their magickal properties in mind, aligning them with your intentions.

(continued)

Safe-to-Burn Herbs for Your Bouquets

Some herbs produce toxic smoke when burned, so always do your research. You *can* burn:

- rose
- lavender
- mugwort
- garden sage
- mint
- dandelion
- rosemary

- basil
- pine needles
- apple blossoms
- blue spruce needles
- Eastern red cedar needles
- juniper

- bay leaf
- mullein
- sweetfern
- lemongrass
- calendula
- lilac
- lemon balm

- chamomile
- catnip
- dill
- thyme
- amaranth
- eucalyptus

Making Smoke-Cleansing Bouquets

CLEANSING AND PURIFYING: pine needles, lavender, rosemary, sage, mint, yarrow

PSYCHIC POWER: mugwort, lavender, roses, yarrow

HEALTH AND HEALING: mint, roses, sage (grief support), pine needles

LOVE AND FRIENDSHIP: basil, lavender, roses, yarrow, pine needles

LUCK: mint, basil, pine needles, dandelion leaves

HAPPINESS AND HARMONY: lavender, mint, basil, sage

INSIGHT AND CLARITY: lavender, rose, mint, rosemary, sage, pine needles

STRENGTH AND VITALITY: mugwort, yarrow, lavender, sage, dandelion leaf, pine needles

Creating the bouquet is satisfying and easy. I wilt the plants for a day before making the bundles, to remove some of the initial moisture and to speed up the drying process.

Start by playing with design, and once you have something you think is beautiful, trim the stems evenly and tie the herbs into a bundle. I use cotton baker's twine. Hemp works well, too.

Wrap the bundle tightly at the base. You'll first want to secure the string with a knot, leaving some slack. Go around the base a few times before proceeding. Wrap the string tightly up the stems in a diagonal fashion. Wrap it once or twice around the top, then come back down at a diagonal in the opposite direction, making a crisscross pattern. Once you get to the bottom, tie it to the slack string. Allow your bouquet to dry on a screen, in a basket, or hanging upside down, for 1 to 2 weeks. Keep the bundle out of sunlight, as it will fade your flora.

HOW TO SAFELY BURN YOUR BOUQUET

When your bouquet is fully dry, light the top. Once you get a decent flame going, blow it out and allow it to smolder and smoke over a heatproof dish or abalone shell, which will catch your hot ashes. The bundle needs airflow to continue burning, so keep it moving, use your breath, or fan it with a feather or your hand. If you do not wish to burn it in its entirety, tamp out the bundle in your heatproof container. You can always use a little water if you are in a hurry, but some practitioners believe this displeases the fire spirits.

Ritual Baths

The Element of Water soothes, cleanses, purifies, and rejuvenates. When combined with healing herbs and spiritual purpose in a ritual bath, it can deliver a powerful, meaningful, and magickal experience. These rituals can be simple, everyday acts, or they can be more elaborate and symbolic. They might celebrate an occasion or mark an event. No matter its purpose, a ritual should always make you feel connected to and a part of something.

CAUTION: Please review plant cautions on page 9 and do your research to ensure safe use.

Milk Bath Basic Recipe

Makes enough for 4 baths

> 4 to 5 tablespoons (10 to 20 g) dried herbs (See page 173 for herb blend possibilities.)
> 1 cup (128 g) powdered milk (I use powdered goat milk, but you can also use cow, coconut, or oat powdered milk.)
> ½ cup (112 g) Epsom salt
> ½ cup (120 g) baking soda

Crush the herbs in your mortar and pestle. In a bowl, combine them with the milk, Epsom salt, and baking soda. Mix well and break up any clumps. Store in an airtight jar. Put the formulation in the refrigerator for a day or two right after you make it, as it infuses the scents of the herbs and spices into the dry ingredients. Use ½ cup (84 g) for your ritual bath. These make wonderful gifts!

Wheel of the Year Ritual Baths

The witch's Wheel of the Year consists of eight sabbats—four solar events called "quarters" in the form of solstices and equinoxes, and four "cross-quarters" that fall in between the solar events. We mark them with celebrations that include food, crafts, community, some introspective time, and acts of self-care. To learn more about the Wheel of the Year, see page 31.

A sabbat ritual bath is a perfect way to root into the meaning of each sabbat, feel a sense of connection with nature and its cycles, and recognize that you are an integral part of this natural cycle of life. It's also a traditional way to purify and prepare yourself for any sabbat-related magickal workings. Adapt the basic milk bath to each sabbat by including herbs and spices. Even if you don't observe the witch's Wheel of the Year, think of them instead as seasonal baths.

Herb and Spice Blends for Each Sabbat Ritual Bath

SAMHAIN (October 31 to November 1, the witch's New Year, cross-quarter): rosemary, mugwort, calendula, and a pinch of pumpkin pie spice (cinnamon, nutmeg, ginger, cloves, allspice).

YULE (December 20 to 23, Winter Solstice): pine needles, finely chopped dried orange peel, and pinches of nutmeg, cinnamon, and ginger.

IMBOLC (February 1, first cross-quarter of the calendar year): sprigs of pine, Eastern red cedar, and/or juniper, vanilla beans, and a pinch of cinnamon.

OSTARA (March 20 to 22, Spring Equinox): lavender, apple blossoms, dandelion blossoms, and lemon balm.

BELTANE (April 30 to May 1, cross-quarter): red or white clover, dandelion blossoms, plantain, and mint.

LITHA (June 20 to 23, Summer Solstice): rose petals, lavender, chamomile, daisy blossoms, and finely chopped dried lemon peel.

LAMMAS DAY OR LUGHNASADH (August 1, cross-quarter): yarrow leaves and blossoms, basil, comfrey, and finely chopped dried grapefruit peel.

MABON (September 20 to 23, Autumn Equinox): sage, mugwort, and a pinch of apple pie spice (cinnamon, nutmeg, allspice).

Black Salt

Salt is a sacred mineral of the Earth with magickal energies that are purifying, protective, and can attract abundance and prosperity. Black salt, often called *Witches' Salt*, is helpful for protection and driving away unwanted negative energy, its properties amplified by its added layer of color magick.

Black salt is made by mixing ash with salt. You can use ash from the fireplace or wood stove and/or from the charred remains of herbal incense. I create my black salt by mixing sea salt (any coarse salt will do) with ashes from our wood stove and ashes left over from burning herbal incense. I use ashes from dried herbs that have cleansing and protection magickal qualities, such as lavender, mint, basil, rosemary, garden sage, mugwort, rose, and pine.

Start by mixing a little ash into a handful of the salt. Slowly add more ash until you achieve the desired tint. I add the tiniest bit of safflower oil to the mixture (any carrier oil or essential oil will do)—just a few drops so the ash readily adheres to the salt, giving it its black color without dissolving the salt or rendering it oily. Another possibility is to mix the salt and ash in your cast-iron cauldron over a tea light, allowing the low heat to combine the two.

CAUTION: Black salt is not to be ingested.

USING BLACK SALT IN YOUR MAGICKAL PRACTICE

- Create a salt circle of protection for spellwork or divination practice.
- Use black salt as an ingredient of protection in a spell jar (page 159).
- Cleanse magickal tools and crystals by sprinkling black salt near them.
- Place a small bag of the salt in your home to absorb negative energies.
- Place a small bag of the salt at the entryway to your home for protection.
- Put a small bag of the salt under your bed to ward off nightmares.
- Use black salt for purification and protection spells.

Cauldron Simmering Potpourri

I am fond of concocting herbal potpourris in my cast-iron cauldron, warming and simmering them over a tealight. These aromatic blends delight the senses and contain magickal properties that can amplify your spellwork. I'll share with you my favorite blends for Samhain and Yule. If you do not observe the Wheel of the Year (page 31), these blends coincide with autumn/Halloween and the Winter Solstice.

Samhain Blend

Magickal properties and associations: psychic powers, divination, astral projection, spirit communication, vivid visions, remembrance, ancestors, Samhain.

Mugwort, rosemary, apple slices
1 to 2 cinnamon sticks
A sprinkling of pumpkin pie spice (cinnamon, nutmeg, ginger, cloves, allspice)

Focus on your intention as you add each ingredient to your cauldron. Use this to enhance the energies required for divination and connecting with spirits beyond the veil.

Yule Blend

Magickal properties and associations: love, joy, healing, renewal, Yule.

Fresh pine sprigs
Apple and citrus slices (orange, lemon, lime, or grapefruit)
Dash of vanilla extract
Handful of fresh cranberries
1 to 2 cinnamon sticks
A few pinches of each of ground or whole cloves, nutmeg, and cardamom

As you indulge in the ritual of crafting this blend, envision the simple things in your life that bring you pleasure and joy, and give thanks for them. As the aromas of the herbs waft into the air, feel your high-vibration energies of joy and gratitude filling up the sacred space of your home.

Flying Ointment

This herbal "flying" ointment recipe is safe, nontoxic, and nonhallucinogenic. It can aid you in your practices of meditation, divination (with tarot reading, scrying, runes, and so forth), spirit communication, and hedge riding (page 179). It can also promote restful sleep and vivid dreaming. The herbs are carefully selected for their magickal properties that relax the body and mind, boost intuition and psychic awareness, provide protection, and clear any negative energies.

I infuse mugwort, yarrow, rose petals, mint, and lavender separately in their own oil, every year with fresh-wilted plant matter and by slow "cool" method, and then combine them for this recipe. For convenience's sake, you can combine them to infuse into your carrier oil, following either the "warm" slow method or Crock-Pot method (both for dried plant matter) on pages 133 to 134.

CAUTION: Please review plant cautions on page 9 and do your research to ensure safe use.

Makes approximately nine 1-ounce (28-g) salves

1 cup (235 ml) herb-infused oil (I use olive oil for this recipe, but you can use any carrier oil.)

¼ cup (40 g) beeswax pastilles or shavings (For a softer consistency, use a little less than ¼ cup.)

20 to 30 drops of essential oils (optional)

Combine all the ingredients except the essential oils in a double boiler. Simmer over low heat, stirring occasionally, until the beeswax melts into the oil. Be careful not to introduce any water into the oil, as it will render the ointment unusable.

note

Vegan options include soy wax and carnauba wax, although there are known ethical harvesting issues with carnauba wax.

For this I like a combination of 13 to 15 drops of lavender, 8 to 10 of sweet orange, and 3 to 5 of patchouli.

The Origins of Flying Ointment

In the sixteenth and seventeenth centuries, some witches greased their brooms with mind-altering hallucinogenic ointments and absorbed them into their bodies to achieve the "flying" state, using poisonous herbs such as belladonna, henbane, and mandrake. Not only was this extremely dangerous but it prevented recall of the experience.

CAUTION: Never use poisonous plants in an herbal preparation.

Once the beeswax has fully melted into the oil, dip a clean spoon into the preparation and place it in the freezer for about a minute. If you like its consistency, you are all set to pour it into your containers. If it feels too soft, melt a little more wax into the warm ointment, and if it feels too hard, add a little bit more of your infused oil. Stir in the essential oils (if using) just before pouring it into your containers.

Optionally, you may adorn your ointment with dried plant matter such as rose petals, a single rosebud, or lavender buds.

TO APPLY THE OINTMENT: Massage a pea-sized amount into your wrists, back of the neck, temples, over the Third Eye, and into the soles of the feet a half hour before your spiritual practice. Store your ointment in a cool, dry place for up to 1 year.

Hedge Riding

The hedge is the boundary between the earthly realm and the Spirit World. Hedge riding is a journey of spirit to receive guidance, knowledge, and healing. You mentally/spiritually "fly" to each realm (Upper, Middle, and Lower) through a portal. I enter through a favorite tree, and others commonly enter through a door, cave, or gateway.

When you practice hedge riding, your mind/spirit is in the Otherworld, yet you know your earthly experience and can come back fully to your body at any time. It's different from visualization, where you have full control and creative license. It's similar to meditation, where you observe, get out of your own way, and allow the journey to unfold without interference.

The Lower World is the easiest to access and my favorite realm to visit. It's an earthly place filled with natural beauty and glorious seasons. You'll meet animal helpers, nature spirits, people, archetypes of the Collective Unconscious and spirit guides. It's a wonderful place to receive answers to straightforward questions and even do spellwork.

To learn more, I recommend Harmonia Saille's *Pagan Portals—Hedge Riding*. It's a wonderful publication, and one that I've used as a guide to inform my own practice.

Magickal Mist

This potion performs double duty, cleansing with properties that will clean, disinfect, and deodorize your home and having magickal qualities associated with home blessings, protection, purification, and the cleansing of negative energy. I use it just as I would any all-purpose cleaner: to wipe down countertops, appliances, and cabinets, to clean bathrooms with, and as a floor wash. The scent of the apple cider vinegar dissipates as it dries. It's satisfying to clean your home while ridding it of negative energies and attracting blessings.

Makes about 4 cups (1 L)

Fresh-wilted lavender, sage, and rosemary
   (You can also make one with pine needles.)
Dehydrated orange peel

1 part apple cider vinegar
1 part distilled water

TO MAKE HERB-INFUSED VINEGAR: Fill a clean quart-size (1-L) mason jar with herbs and dried orange peel. Leave 1 inch (2.5 cm) of headspace. If using dried plant matter, fill the jar halfway. Pour apple cider vinegar over the herbs to the top of the jar and cap it with a nonreactive, noncorrosive lid. Place it in a warm spot, out of direct sunlight for 4 to 6 weeks. Strain out plant matter. Pour the liquid into a clean quart-size jar and label it.

TO MAKE MAGICKAL MIST: Combine 1 cup (235 ml) of herb-infused apple cider vinegar with 1 cup (235 ml) of distilled water in a spray bottle.

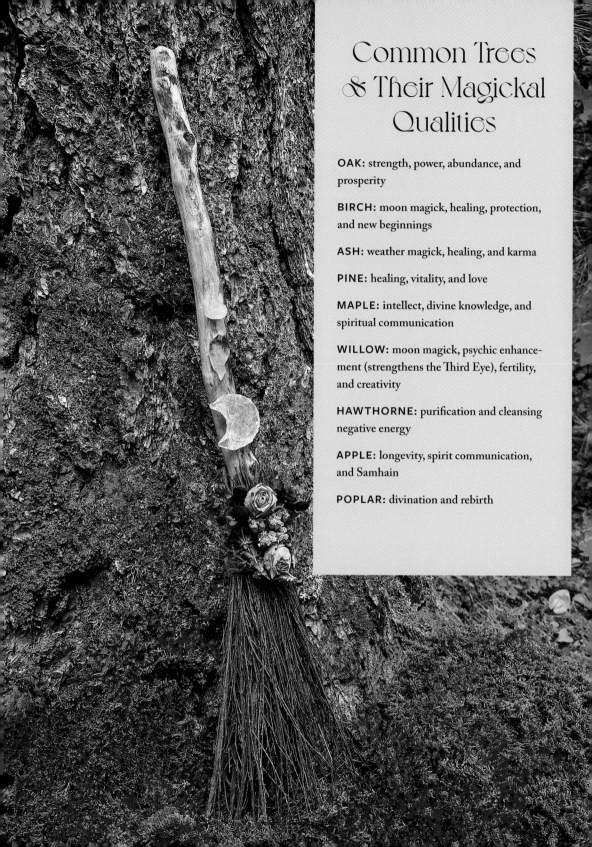

Common Trees & Their Magickal Qualities

OAK: strength, power, abundance, and prosperity

BIRCH: moon magick, healing, protection, and new beginnings

ASH: weather magick, healing, and karma

PINE: healing, vitality, and love

MAPLE: intellect, divine knowledge, and spiritual communication

WILLOW: moon magick, psychic enhancement (strengthens the Third Eye), fertility, and creativity

HAWTHORNE: purification and cleansing negative energy

APPLE: longevity, spirit communication, and Samhain

POPLAR: divination and rebirth

Witch's Broom (Besom)

I wildcraft many a witch's broom, called a *besom*, out of twigs, branches, dried grasses, and roots from the forest outside my door. I use parts of the trees that have fallen to the ground, so as not to harm a live tree and expose it to disease or insects. Most besoms that I wildcraft are small, so they can easily fit on my altar or on the small round table with other magickal tools, where I conduct my magickal workings.

Besoms are used to "sweep" away negative energies from one's home, to cleanse a space before doing magickal work, or to brush away any negative energies from around your aura or someone else's aura. Removing the negative and unwanted energies makes room for beneficial energies. The head of the besom does not actually touch the ground as we make this sweep.

Different types of wood have unique magickal properties. I allow the wood to choose me. Swamp maple, pine, and birch seem to find me. If you dwell in the city or suburbia, visit your local park after a strong windstorm to find fallen branches.

The wood you use will impart specific magickal energies as you use your broom, and if you wish to charge it further, you can adorn it with herbs and crystals. To increase your besom's ability to cleanse and purify a space, consider adorning it with rosemary, lavender, mint, sage, mugwort, or pine. You might also consider weaving in some herbs that support and amplify psychic ability, so that as you sweep away negative energies before doing your magickal work, you increase the energies required for divination and spellwork. Herbs that increase psychic power include lavender, mint, basil, dandelion, mugwort, clover, rose, yarrow, and apple. I like to include chips of amethyst to amplify psychic ability and bits of rose quartz for unconditional love from the Universe.

Wildcrafted Witch's Broom

Before putting your besom together, make sure that the twigs or grass bundles for the head of the broom are of equal length. Depending on their thickness, you can either use a scissor or a small hand saw to cut them. If you don't mind the natural look, and if the branches and twigs are quite dry, you can simply snap them with your fingers. You can always smooth their tips with sandpaper, if you'd like.

To make small ritual brooms, you can simply place either twigs, roots, or grass around a main small branch "handle" and secure it with twine. For more stability, you can secure each twig (or root, or tuft of grass) to the main branch with a dot of hot glue.

For medium to large brooms, weave twine, cord, or a leather strip into the twigs, securing them to the handle using an over/under approach and some hot glue. For larger brooms, you can also incorporate a few tiny nails to attach the cord to the broom handle.

Crystal and Herb Grid Magick

Crystal grids are powerful energy tools of sacred geometry that will aid you in realizing your dreams, goals, and intentions. They are a form of spellwork, really. The origins of sacred geometry patterns are found in the mysterious, harmonic architecture of Ancient Egypt, built in perfect proportion to mimic, express, honor, and make sense of the divine plan that underlies the natural world.

Crystal grids draw from ancient geometric patterns. Common templates include the "Seed of Life" and the "Flower of Life," both formed by interlocking circles. The potency of the crystal grid comes from the collective energy created by the healing stones that are placed together on the grid. As a green witch, I naturally incorporate herbs into my crystal grids, ones that complement the magickal properties of the crystals. You can use actual grids (printed on wood, cloth, or paper) or create them freeform on a flat surface, or even on your body.

USING YOUR CRYSTAL GRID

Choose your crystals, herbs, and patterns. You will need 5 to 13 crystals/herbs (or more, depending on your grid). These can be as intricate or as simplistic as you'd like. Begin by thinking of your intention and selecting 1 or 2 types of crystals and 1 or 2 herbs with properties that correspond with your intention. (Review the plant profiles to see which one[s] correspond with your intention.) For example, if your intention is focused on healing, you might choose clear quartz and rose quartz crystals, rosebuds, and pinecones.

Cleanse the grid and crystals before composing your layout, perhaps by passing them through some incense smoke.

There is no right or wrong way to create a pattern on the grid, and it is a good idea to focus on your intention while you build it. Start by placing a power stone in the center—whichever crystal you deem to be the strongest. This is called the *master crystal* or *anchor crystal*.

Following your intuition, place the remaining crystals and herbs on the grid in a pattern that resonates with you. Charge and activate your grid by envisioning the master crystal's energy radiating out, connecting all the individual crystals and herbs, the connection magnifying their power and magickal potential. Envision your intentions becoming one with the arrangement.

Place your finished crystal grid in a special location—maybe on your altar. Leave it be for whatever amount of time feels right. Sometimes I create one before engaging in spellwork or a divination practice, and then I dismantle it once I'm done. If I've created a grid to help foster creativity for a project, I'll leave it up for the duration of the project.

RESOURCES

BOOKS ABOUT WITCHCRAFT

Diaz, Juliet. *Witchery: Embrace the Witch Within*. Hay House, 2019.

Grossman, Pam. *Waking the Witch: Reflections on Women, Magic, and Power*. Gallery Books, 2019.

Herstik, Gabriela. *Inner Witch: A Modern Guide to the Ancient Craft*. TarcherPerigee, 2018.

Spalter, Mya. *Enchantments: A Modern Guide to Self-Possession*. Lenny, 2018.

Tempest Zakroff, Laura. *Weave the Liminal: Living Modern Traditional Witchcraft*. Llewelyn Publications, 2019.

Any book by Silver RavenWolf.

EDUCATIONAL RESOURCES

The Herbal Academy: theherbalacademy.com

LearningHerbs: learningherbs.com

The Chestnut School of Herbal Medicine: chestnutherbs.com

BOOKS ABOUT SPELLWORK AND DIVINATION

Ahlquist, Diane. *Moon Magic: Your Complete Guide to Harnessing the Mystical Energy of the Moon*. Adams Media, 2017.

Alexander, Skye. *The Modern Witchcraft Book of Tarot: Your Complete Guide to Understanding the Tarot*. Adams Media, 2017.

Auryn, Mat. *Psychic Witch: A Metaphysical Guide to Meditation, Magick & Manifestation*. Llewellyn Publications, 2020.

Dean, Liz. *The Ultimate Guide to Divination: The Beginner's Guide to Using Cards, Crystals, Runes, Palmistry, and More for Insight and Predicting the Future*. Fair Winds Press, 2018.

Greenleaf, Cerridwen. *The Practical Witch's Spell Book for Love, Happiness, and Success*. Running Press, 2018.

Murphy-Hiscock, Arin. *Spellcrafting: Strengthen the Power of Your Craft by Creating and Casting Your Own Unique Spells*. Adams Media, 2020.

Saille, Harmonia. *Pagan Portals— Hedge Riding*. Moon Books, 2012.

Wright, Sandra Mariah and Leanne Marrama. *Reading the Leaves: An Intuitive Guide to the Ancient Art and Modern Magic of Tea Leaf Divination*. TarcherPerigee, 2020.

BOOKS ABOUT PLANTS, HERBALISM, AND FORAGING

Bennett, Robin Rose. *The Gift of Healing Herbs: Plant Medicines and Home Remedies for a Vibrantly Healthy Life*. North Atlantic Books, 2014.

Cunningham, Scott. *Cunningham's Encyclopedia of Magickal Herbs*. Llewellyn Publications, 2019.

Gladstar, Rosemary. *Rosemary Gladstar's Medicinal Herbs: A Beginner's Guide*. Storey Publishing, 2012.

Graham, April. *Spare Changing for Trauma: A Memoir of Pain & Healing*. Self-published via Docucopies, 2019.

Hardin, Kiva Rose. *A Weedwife's Remedy: Folk Herbalism for the Hedgewise*. Plant Healer Press, 2019.

Kimmerer, Robin Wall. *Braiding Sweetgrass: Indigenous Wisdom, Scientific Knowledge, and the Teachings of Plants*. Milkweed Editions, 2013.

Meredith, Leda. *The Skillful Forager: Essential Techniques for Responsible Foraging and Making the Most of Your Wild Edibles*. Roost Books, 2019.

DRIED HERBS

Frontier Co-op: frontiercoop.com

Mountain Rose Herbs: mountainroseherbs.com

BOTTLES, JARS, AND TINS

Berlin Packaging: berlinpackaging.com

Specialty Bottle: specialtybottle.com

ACKNOWLEDGMENTS

Deepest gratitude and respect to everyone at Fair Winds Press/The Quarto Group, especially to Jill Alexander for her visions for this book and believing in this work, and Jenna Nelson Patton for transforming the manuscript into a book with all her help, care, editing expertise, and attention to detail. Many thanks also goes to Anne Re, Meredith Quinn, Lydia Anderson, Amy Paradysz, Winnie Prentiss, and all the talented people at Quarto who made the release of this book possible.

Big thanks to an ever-growing list of souls who have inspired my work and Craft—individuals whose work serves the greater good through the arenas of witchcraft, family herbalism, foraging, and environmental stewardship: the late Scott Cunningham and Zora Neale Hurston, Laurie Cabot, Ann Moura, Pam Grossman, Laura Tempest Zakroff, Arin Murphy-Hiscock, Robin Wall Kimmerer, Kiva Rose Hardin, David Spahr, Leda Meredith, Rosemary Gladstar, Robin Rose Bennett, Katrina Blair, Susun Weed, April Graham, Deb Soule, and those I have yet to learn from.

Many thanks to my family—Howie, Elijah, and Rose—for helping to provide a calm and quiet working environment for me as I labored on this book during COVID quarantine and remote work/school time.

Special thanks to Ike and Grace for their love, guidance, and assistance.

Much gratitude to fellow kindreds I've met via Instagram, for their support, kindness, and enthusiastic requests for me to share about green witchcraft within the context of a book. I'm happy to be able to present this one to you. And big thanks to you, the reader, for your interest in this book. I hope you will find it to be of value as you explore your own unique path.

ABOUT THE AUTHOR

SUSAN ILKA TUTTLE is a green witch, folk herbalist, psychic medium and spirit messenger, and photo artist living in the woods of Maine with her husband and two children. In the Wood Botanicals is her small-batch herbalism business through which she offers wildcrafted, plant-based body care products. Susan believes that when we work in concert with plants, transforming them into medicinal and magickal blends, we awaken an inner knowing within and are gifted with an opportunity to reclaim our forgotten, deep-rooted, and fundamental relationship to safe, simple plant allies that nourish, heal, and restore us. In return, we strive to preserve and protect Her limited resources. Susan is excited to assist you on your personal journey of connecting (reconnecting) with the plants. *Green Witch Magick* is her fifth book.

CONNECT WITH SUSAN

inthewoodbotanicals.com
susantuttlespiritmessenger.com
Instagram: @whisper_in_the_wood

INDEX